**LOSS,
LOVE AND LESSONS**

Healing pet loss and grief

Also by this author:

Heartbreak, Healing and Happiness: Flourishing after a heartbreak
Grief, Grace and Gratitude: Transforming through your grief journey

LOSS, LOVE AND LESSONS

Healing pet loss and grief

LARA CASANOVA

Loss, Love and Lessons
Author – Lara Casanova

© Lara Casanova 2020

www.lifeinthepink.com.au
lara@lifeinthepink.com.au

This book is sold with the understanding that the author is not offering specific personal advice to the reader. For professional advice, seek the services of a suitable qualified practitioner. The author disclaims any responsibility for liability, loss or risk, personal or otherwise, that happens as a consequence of the use and application of any of the contents of this book.

All rights reserved. This book may not be reproduced in whole or part, stored, posted on the internet, or transmitted in any form or by any means, electronic, mechanical, photocopying, recording, or other, without permission from the author of this book.

Editing and design by: www.authorsupportservices.com
Photography by: www.realmomentsphotography.com.au

ISBN: 978-1-922375-03-2

A catalogue record for this book is available from the National Library of Australia

To
Max
Holmcroft Bopix Frazer

Maxy, Maxo,
My main man,
My best friend,
My beautiful baby boy,

You left a zillion paw prints on my heart!
17.7.99 - 22.6.14
and
All his friends at Rainbow Bridge!

"A true friend leaves paw prints on your heart."

—Unknown

Foreword

I have known Lara Casanova for many years through our mutual work within the veterinary industry. Now we have reconnected through our joint experience of losing our pets, and the devastating grief that followed. We have both felt called, in our own ways, to share our experiences to help other grieving pet owners move through, and heal from, their loss. As a result, Lara has created this beautiful book *Loss, Love and Lessons – Healing pet loss and grief*.

Each grief experience is unique. All too often owners are unprepared for the emotions they experience. Reading other pet owners' stories is a wonderful way to feel connected through your grief. In part one, Lara's Max narrates his story through his eyes, and then Lara shares the story from her perspective. Reading these stories left me in tears as I contemplated again the life and loss of my Toby and Milly.

Toby was a born performer and loved to be the centre of attention. My best friend, he went everywhere with me. Losing him was extremely difficult. It was a sad and lonely time. Sometimes I felt like I couldn't breathe, almost like I was going crazy in my grief. I wish this book had been published then as it would have absolutely held space for me to delve into and heal my grief, and honour it and Toby even more.

Lara certainly provides a soft place for anyone to land as they work through their grief journey. She has a real grasp on what can arise when we lose our pets and the intense bond of love that we have with them. Through her personal loss journey, her extensive experience in the veterinary industry and professional studies, she is the perfect person to write this book.

True to the woman Lara is, she really opens her heart in this book, inviting readers to connect though her story to their own grief in need of healing. She provides an amazing love-grief toolbox and details the stages of grief, so pet owners know what to expect and how to deal with what arises. Lara is very cognisant that different things work for different people and thus provides many options for readers to choose from. She gives ideas for tributes, memorials and rituals and even how to help children heal.

Like Lara, I have felt that pet grief is invariably misunderstood. There has certainly been a shift in the last twenty years, but I believe our society still needs to be more open to, and understand more, the depth and profundity of pet loss and grief. This book goes a long way to achieving this.

Loss, Love and Lessons is really such a lovely book that will honour your pet and your grief. I highly recommend it to help you on your grief journey. I will leave you with Lara's words that particularly touched me: "Two souls connected as one, holding a love that never dies" and "The whole point is Love!"

Dr Katrina Warren
Media Veterinarian and Presenter
Founder, Wonderdog School

Insta @drkatrina
FB @Dr Katrina

Preface

"Dogs come into our lives to teach us about love. They depart to teach us about loss. A new dog never replaces an old dog; it merely expands the heart. If you have loved many dogs, your heart is very big."

—Erica Jong

The journey through pet loss and grief can be a long, winding, misunderstood and tumultuous road. It is also a beautiful and heartfelt love story of two souls connected as one, holding a love that never dies.

The aftermath of losing your pet can be overwhelming. Heartbreaking. An intense sense of emptiness, sorrow and aloneness may encase you as you now live in a world devoid of those familiar quirks that hallmarked your pet. Maybe it is their toenails tapping down the hallway, their wet nose at your feet while you prepare dinner, their sad eyes looking at you when you leave the house or their fur over all your clothes. Perhaps it is simply that the beautiful wispy air of love is no longer hot on your heels wherever you go.

Your days are altered. The energy that rises in the house when the afternoon walk time approaches is no longer there, and the pleading energy waiting at your feet is unbearably missed. You may have another dog to continue with your routine, but the absence of one is noticeable. Your walk is shrouded by sadness.

Perhaps you feel the loss of a wonderful source of emotional comfort. The loneliness, and for some even the depression and anxiety they had before their pet joined their family, starts creeping back. We can simply feel lost. Everything seems to have changed.

Why is it that pet grief cuts so deep? We expect to feel shattered, but the depth of our despair can surprise us. With few people to talk to who truly understand our anguish, we can easily become cloaked with a deep sense of loss and are clueless on how to proceed, how to grieve, how to say goodbye and how to honour our loss.

Pet loss is a form of disenfranchised grief that it is not recognised well by our society. For those of us who have lost pets, our grief is often dismissed or minimised, seriously affecting our ability to move through it in a healthy fashion. People belittle pet grief and, without understanding, allude to it being mystifying or unwarranted. They can even invalidate it. This can lead a mourner to suppress their feelings and dismiss their grief in an unhealthy fashion. Others may hide out at home, hoping to find some alone time to honour their pet and their feelings without the negative distraction of others.

Everyone handles their grief differently. The way you grieve for one pet too can differ to how you grieve for another. Your pet, your grief and your story will be different to mine but similar in that your heart feels broken, bereft and empty.

It's important to honour your expression of loss as it presents while being careful of others' opinions, especially the negative ones that diminish your grief. To add fuel to the fire, well-meaning people and societal conditioning may pressure you to hurry your grief: to stop talking about it, stop crying, get over it, get another pet and move on. A flurry of inappropriate though well-intentioned

Preface

comments may come your way. Tactless delivery or poor choice of words can add more insult to your fragile heart.

Sadly, all this is not always easy. It certainly wasn't for me and it hasn't been for the numerous people I have met over my many years working in the veterinary (vet) industry. Many of those seeking help with their pet loss and grief often cannot find a reputable counsellor skilled in the intricacies of pet grief. This type of grief can have us contemplating other forms of grief, our own mortality or even the meaning of life.

Everyone has a different relationship with their pet. For some, like me, our pets are much more than a pet; they are the equivalent to a human child in our eyes and treated accordingly. For others, they are loyal friends and, as the Australians (Aussies) call them, their 'best mate'. Maybe they are the last link to a deceased relative, our only form of social interaction, a reason to get up in the morning, someone to take care of, a therapy dog, our childhood sweetheart, our workmate, our therapist, our movie-watching couch potato friend, our walking buddy, our jogging friend, our best friend, our travel companion, our humour source, our true love or all of the above rolled into one furry, feathery or scaly ball.

Our pets teach us many lessons and the biggest is about unconditional love! Looking deeply into a fur child's soft, innocent and vulnerable eyes takes you straight to a pure, beautiful soul. One that will do anything for you. Loyal to the core and faithful till the end, your pet's only desire is to serve your every need and please you, the one they love.

No words are needed to appreciate the depth of the love we find when we look into our pet's eyes. This love is beamed straight into our hearts, entwining with our own love and opening our hearts to experience the grandest, most beautiful love.

This unconditional love is so deeply entrenched, it's no wonder we struggle to move past their passing. We all seek this magical and beautiful love and yearn to replicate the relationships we have with animals with the humans in our life. Sadly we are often let down as the human condition comes into play. Human relationships are so much more complicated. Animals ask much less but often provide so much more. So, often we may cling and pour our energy, love and soul into our relationship with our pets and bask in the joy and love they sprinkle over our lives.

Pets provide unconditional love.

When the day comes to say goodbye, your fragile heart is shattered. You stand alone, confused, crushed and deeply grieving. How do you say goodbye to a furry friend that brings us to this special place of deep, unconditional, untainted love? It's like no other love except maybe that with our children. Even then, unfortunately, it's not always the case. With our pets, there are no judgements, attachments or expectations placed on the relationship. It's one of unadulterated love. As this love is so hard to replicate through the human-to-human experience, it is part of the reason why saying goodbye is so agonising, and the depth of grief can be unlike anything we have experienced before. We berate ourselves for struggling so much, adding to the depth of our suffering. The inability of others to relate to this type of grief can add to the sense of feeling very alone. That's one reason I wrote this book. So you are not alone.

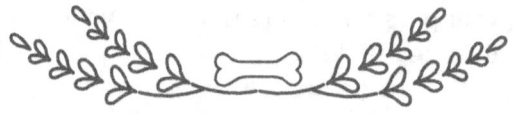

Loss, Love and Lessons takes you on a step-by-step journey through the valleys, peaks and all the in-betweens of pet grief while you face the raw pain. Essentially, this book guides you through the heartfelt love story of loss and grief as you say goodbye to your pet, uncovering the love that awaits you at the other end of the journey and allows you to appreciate the lessons your pet gifts you on their passing.

Preface

Loss, Love and Lessons will also help you to:

- 🐾 journey through the heartfelt loss and grief
- 🐾 follow the loving paw prints made by your pet on your heart to the deep love within
- 🐾 know that two souls are connected as one, holding a love that never dies
- 🐾 heal your loss, feel the love and appreciate the lessons, knowing that *the whole point is love!*

The process is slow, sometimes very slow, and very lonely. It takes time to walk the footsteps through this pain, yet it can be so rewarding as you honour your pet, the love you hold, and the two souls connected as one forever.

Without grief there is no love. To heal through the grief leaves a love so deep, and this love cracks open your heart. This enables you to remember your beloved pet and touch daily the love that shines down brightly from your angel who has crossed over the Rainbow Bridge. This is the mythical bridge that I believe connects heaven and Earth, and it is where we pet owners will reunite with our departed friends one day.

I am an absolute animal lover. I'm sure you can tell! I am the girl who walks down the street anywhere in the world and stops to talk to every dog! My family and friends now just keep walking and laugh as I squat and speak through the animal's eyes and directly to their soul. I run my fingers through their silky coats, asking the owners all sorts of questions about their special fur child. Being surrounded by animals makes my day – correction, my life! I have a sense that part of my life dharma is to watch out for all the animals – big, small, furry, feathery or scaly. I even place millipedes from my shower back in the garden. Carrying this dharma is a big task and not for the faint-hearted, but it recoups great rewards. So, I am incredibly lucky!

Loss, Love and Lessons

For fourteen years I worked in the vet industry as a business manager for a few clinics – one very big multi-clinic organisation and one smaller, boutique one. I deeply loved both my roles. While mostly being in my office and helping run the business and staff, I was also very involved in the animals' wellbeing while they were with us at the clinic, being present with many as they transitioned to Rainbow Bridge.

When owners could not stay with their pets at this difficult time, I stepped in and sat with them, held their paws, fed them treats, reiterated what a good pet they were, and sent them off with arms filled with love on their journey to the next realm. In the later years, I also secretly sent with each one a special message for my boy Max who this book is dedicated to and inspired by. I believe no one should ever leave this Earth feeling scared and alone, and our pets are no exception.

I have sat with owners, discussed the euthanasia process with them and held their hands while they said goodbye to their family member. Each time is heartbreaking, often with racking sobs echoing throughout the clinic. The depth of love is apparent in each case and the very real distress the owners feel must be managed gently. Each vulnerable heart needs a delicate and soft place to land. Leaving the veterinary (vet) clinic with an empty collar and lead is traumatic.

Yet, this is the grief that is often repressed as society does not see it as important or as necessary as human grief. This is so far from the truth. Ask any true animal lover!

Never ever apologise for the depth of your grief over your pet loss. When your heart spills, allow it to flow like a majestic river through your soul and follow the paw prints of love on your heart as you honour yourself and your pet. Your grief is very real and demonstrates the love you hold for your pet, which deserves all the tears. It's your open and grieving heart that allows you to feel this so deeply. Never excuse this vulnerable and beautiful part of yourself to appease society and those who do not understand,

Preface

appreciate or have a heart so big to have experienced such profound love.

I too have experienced this journey of love and loss. My golden retriever, Max, my golden fur angel, crossed to the Rainbow Bridge in June 2014. Our story is one of two souls connected as one, holding tightly to a love that will never die! He certainly left my heart covered in loving paw prints that I followed tenaciously to heal the grief, allowing my heart to break wide open to reveal the pure love. Through sharing our story and all the heart spills along the way – my loss, my love and my lessons when I walked the tough journey – I hope you can give yourself permission to follow the paw prints on your heart and to continue with your grieving. I want you to know that it is perfectly normal, and vital, to take this grief journey if you wish to heal and move forward.

> Follow the paw prints on your heart.

When we see ourselves in others' stories we can begin to heal; we don't feel so alone. I hope it comforts you to know there are individuals who understand the grief you feel. Know that you do not need permission from others to grieve, only from yourself. You just need to follow your heart and the paw prints left behind, scattered all over it, which will walk you home to the beautiful, divine love in your heart.

I have studied, gaining qualifications in counselling with an advanced study major in grief and loss, worked in the industry and researched pet grief extensively over the years. But going through the experience myself has by far made me feel even more qualified to help others through this tough time and to share my grief story. My story is built around loving and losing Max, my dog. So I refer to 'furry' a lot. But I love cats, lizards, guinea pigs, pigs and all creatures: you name it, I love it. So no matter if you have lost a furry, feathery or scaly friend, this book is still written for you, despite the references to furry and dog throughout.

Loss, Love and Lessons

Many years later there are still tears. I still miss Max deeply and struggle to understand why dogs live such short lives. I read a saying from a young child recently that went something like this: 'People are born to learn how to love and live a good life. But dogs already know this, so they don't have to stay as long.'

It is upsetting but true. They know in every moment how to live their best life and to love fully, deeply and richly. There are so many gifts and lessons they leave from their short time here that we can adopt to help us live our own lives a little better, a little more connected and open, with a little more love. Pets in all their different forms really are miracles almost akin to a spiritual guru, sent to help us understand this pure, unconditional love.

We are so very lucky to have them in our lives. They deserve the absolute best: food, water, exercise and especially a warm snuggly bed and blankets, treats, kisses, warm baths, beach days, a comfy couch, games, toys galore, adventures, swims, park visits, healthcare and absolutely anything else that spoils them rotten. But most of all they deserve our love, for that is really all that they desire!

Join me on this journey and allow me to share my story. As you reminisce, give permission for your heart spills, find the paw prints and follow them all the way to the love in your heart on your healing journey. Together we can remember the deep, great love of our beautiful fur angels who are shining down on us and sprinkling love on us at every opportunity.

I envision that in between running amuck or just basking in the sun with their newfound health and vigour at Rainbow Bridge, your animal friend often stops and just sits and thinks of their life long ago and the love they have for their best friend and true love: You! They smile and honour this memory with a wag of their tail, a wiggle of their butt and a woof. Then they return to their games, to their life in the moment, happy and joyful. They miss you but they are not sad.

Preface

They know! They fully comprehend that one day you will reunite and know how beautiful it will be. In the meantime they enjoy every moment: the union of your souls is not dependent on geography. The love is unconditional and is always in both hearts, no matter how far apart you now seem to be. I am sure they hope you come to understand this also.

I am certain they are praying that you follow their paw prints of love sprinkled all over your heart, to connect to yourself and your grief, bust your heart wide open with love, and live the richest and fullest life in their honour. A life full of joy and happiness just as they are, while you both wait! Two souls connected as one, forever holding a love that never dies. What an absolute blessing!

I extend my deepest heartfelt condolences to you for your loss. I hope you can find and follow the paw prints on your heart to heal the loss, feel the love and appreciate the lessons.

Contents

Foreword vii
Preface ix
Introduction 1
Pink Pet Tools 7

PART 1
The Loss

My Doggy Life by Max 15
Losing Max 49
The Path of Grief 59

PART 2
The Love

The Love-Grief Dichotomy 77
Loving Grief Models 87
Love and Grief Tools and Strategies 131
Honouring the Love 161

PART 3
The Lessons

Learnings from a Dog's Life: Max's Manifesto 193

Epilogue	247
Appendix	255
Life in the Pink	261
Acknowledgements	265
Extra Resources	267
Other Helpful Links	273

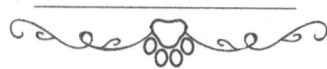

Without grief
there is no love.

"A dog wags his tail with his heart."

—Martin Buxbaum

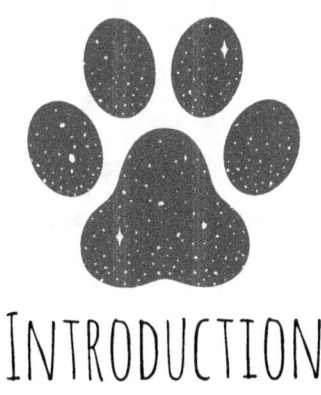

Introduction

> "Whoever said diamonds are a girl's best friend obviously never owned a dog."
>
> —Unknown

Pet loss and grief is a tough and misunderstood journey.

It is a path of healing the loss, feeling the love and appreciating the lessons. With this book, my goal is to provide you with a path forward while supporting you to manoeuvre through this journey using the paw prints left behind that allow your heart to heal.

Loss, Love and Lessons explores grief in all its manifestations and provides you with all you need to move through, process and heal your grief. The structure, different ideas, models, and various strategies and tools will provide you with an opportunity to really be with your grief. It's about not running away from the pain, but walking through it with one end goal in mind: to live with a heart full of the pure, unconditional love you experienced with your pet.

In *Loss, Love and Lessons* you will learn:

- 🐾 what pet grief is and why it hurts so much
- 🐾 why it's important to take the grief journey
- 🐾 how to heal through your loss and move forward

Loss, Love and Lessons

- 🐾 how to help your children through their grief
- 🐾 the strategies, tools and stages of grief
- 🐾 how to process your grief and your feelings
- 🐾 how to deal with others who do not understand
- 🐾 how to find people who do understand
- 🐾 how to access the love that lies below the pain
- 🐾 how to honour your pet, say goodbye and plan a memorial
- 🐾 how to create a tribute or write a eulogy
- 🐾 how to connect to yourself and your grief to feel less alone
- 🐾 to know when it may be time for a new pet
- 🐾 the lessons our pets teach us through their life and their passing.

Our pets have one purpose in life: to love us unconditionally. In turn, they teach us this magical gift alongside many other heartfelt lessons. They model pure, unconditional love to us at every opportunity.

If we stop, look and listen they are a wealth of knowledge on how to live a richer and fuller life. Their presence brings tears, laughter, frustration, disappointment and a rainbow of other emotions.. Mostly they bring us love. It always comes back to the love.

They certainly leave us too soon and leave our heart filled with grief. But the love they radiate once we move through the grief fills up our heart and makes it more beautiful than before. It's just a matter of taking the grief journey when it arrives!

When you walk the grief journey you learn to dive deep into your heart and become intimate with your feelings and emotions – mostly your grief and your love. It is the extent of your love that exacerbates the grief. However, the more you can feel your grief, the more you can feel your love. Walking to the centre of the pain, despite a natural reluctance to avoid it, is absolutely the best thing

INTRODUCTION

you can do for your fragile heart. It will allow your heart to burst open with love later down the grief journey. So, begin to brace yourself to surrender to grief and trust that the paw prints your pet has planted over your heart will lead you through.

Loss, Love and Lessons is made up of three parts.

> Surrender to the grief journey.

Part 1 The Loss mirrors the loss and grief you may be feeling. It has three sections. The first is narrated from the point of view of my golden retriever, Max, from his special place over the Rainbow Bridge. The second is narrated by myself, sharing loss from my perspective.

The third introduces you to the path of grief, the part society plays in diminishing your grief, how your pets are linked to life events and why it is imperative to listen to your grief. Through reading about others' stories, you will know that you are not alone with your grief. Being aware of and listening to others' grief also helps to process your own and moves you towards healing your loss.

Reading Max's story in *Part 1* may draw out sadness and tears, which could well be that necessary catalyst for you to connect and process your own sadness. If, however, it is too raw for you right now, feel free to skip his story and move straight into the self-help section in the part, titled *The Path of Grief*. You might return to his story later when you have more tools and skills to handle the grief that arises.

Part 2 The Love teaches you that without loss and grief there is no love. So as you walk through the loss, you learn how to deal with the devastating grief and the avalanche of emotions while uncovering the love at the end of the grief and loss. It touches on the powerful human-animal bond and the unconditional love your pet gifts you. It details the stages of grief and explains different models of grief, and tools and strategies for dealing with grief, offering you different ideas to honour your love for your pet. It leads you forward through the grief to feel the love.

Part 3 The Lessons is filled with the lessons that are absorbed by your pets and reflected brightly back to you, and those that they teach you indirectly. These all help you to live a richer, fuller life and achieve your highest potential as you move forward and appreciate the lessons.

Three types of content are interwoven throughout this book:

1. self-help information that arms you with tools, exercises and strategies to help you heal your grief.
2. my love story with Max, my golden retriever, through his eyes and my own.
3. the opportunity to revisit your own love story.

Each facet of the content brings you a little deeper and a little closer to your grief and your heart. Once you are connected to your grief you begin to heal and become reconnected to the love.

Everyone will have a different experience of grief, yet you may relate to a part of my story, which may help you to feel less alone through your journey. Pet loss can make you feel even more alone than normal grief due to the way it is viewed in society. So, weaving your way through your journey with a supportive, experienced hand may soften it a little.

As with my two previous books, throughout this book are references to the colour pink. My business was named after a favourite phrase of mine, 'In the Pink', which was coined in the sixteenth century. It means to be strong (physically, mentally, spiritually and emotionally), operating well and in good condition. The colour pink has various other meanings that appeal to me. In the ancient yoga tradition it is related to the heart chakra. It is associated with giving and receiving, producing a calm effect on our energies and helping us to heal. It represents tenderness, care, compassion and unconditional love – just like our pets!

INTRODUCTION

My business and personal values are all based around finding ways to live a life in the pink. I understand that not all people may enjoy pink like I do; colours are personal. If this is true for you just replace pink with whatever colour works with your heart to access the most healing. This is your journey and it is important to individualise it to work for you.

Grief can take all your strength, energy and sanity, so it's important to listen to your body and your heart as you proceed. Go at your own pace and only do what feels right for you at the time. Be gentle with yourself. Notice your energy and rest when needed. Allow each day to unfold as it does without judgement and follow the path, surrendering to the journey. Allow the love to be revealed to you as the grief is processed. Give yourself time.

Unfortunately, the only way to heal the grief journey is to walk its path, despite how difficult and emotionally draining it can be. Find your support people who understand pet grief and call on them when you need help. There is pain but there is also a profound beauty that can be found through this process as it unravels.

Grief can bring profound love and beauty.

Give yourself the gift of the grief journey despite any misgivings. There are so many beautiful things to learn and to remember as you grieve. They are always with you!

My deepest desire for you is to take the journey and walk through the pain to the love that is waiting on the other side. There you will find healing, acceptance and peace. Your furry friend who lives in each moment would want you to enjoy a rich and full life.

So, I invite you to come on the journey with me through *Loss, Love and Lessons*. This journey will leave a love so deep and will allow your heart to fully open. Follow the paw prints on your heart through the grief. Feel the grief, all the heart spills along the way, and find and truly honour the unconditional love of two souls connected as one: you and your pet.

Pink Pet Tools

"A dog can show you more honest affection with a flick of his tail than a man can gather through a lifetime of handshakes."

—Gene Hill

As you travel through your grief journey it is beneficial to learn new tools and strategies that help you to take time out to reflect and contemplate, enabling the navigation of the grief journey to be a little easier and alleviating the sense of feeling lost and alone.

This book is interactive. So, it's in doing the work that you reap the benefits, not just by understanding the theory. To help you on your grief journey, you will notice scattered throughout this book two learning aids:

> 🐾 *Pink Pet Reflections* are exercises that give you an opportunity to express your feelings as you journey through your heartfelt loss and grief. Each time you visit please slow down and stop. Take a few deep breaths to relax the body and the mind, which will help release tension and allow the heart to open and begin the healing journey.
>
> Each time you arrive at a Pink Pet Reflection you will be given a reminder to 'Stop, take a deep breath and reflect. Give yourself permission to go inward, access your Inner

Pink Star (explained below) and the paw prints on your heart. Follow their lead all the way home to the pure, unconditional love of two souls connected as one, holding a love that never dies as you heal your loss, feel the love and appreciate the lessons, knowing that *the whole point is love!*'

🐾 **Pink Pet Love Notes** reflect times in my grief journey and little thoughts I had and still hold onto. These may help you grow closer to your own experiences and feelings.

You will be encouraged to handpick a journal to complete the exercises. Journalling is a wonderful way to become more truthful and intimate with your journey. It is a very cathartic and healing activity. You may like to note your own experiences and feelings as you move through your journey. I refer to this journal as your 'Pink Pet Grief Journal'.

A key to utilising these learning aids is learning to connect to your inner self, your heart – or what I call your Inner Pink Star...

Calling on your Inner Pink Star

I first coined the term 'Inner Pink Star' in *Heartbreak, Healing and Happiness*, referring to the beautiful part inside of you that houses your inner guidance, intuition, inner wisdom or gut instinct. You could simply say 'your heart'. She is a part of you that you may have neglected to listen to sometimes or forgotten. Even so, she is still there quietly in the background, patiently waiting for acknowledgement. You may have overlooked the fact that you always know the answer. Starting to listen to her is where life starts to move you closer to your truth. The three steps forward and one step back starts to become more steps forward. You hear a voice and you know it's your Inner Pink Star.

Pink Pet Tools

When you follow her voice, she leads you to your Inner Creator. Your Inner Creator can pull out your vulnerabilities and sorrow. It can unearth the feelings that lay on the cusp of your heart, yearning to be released and sent out to the world through your Inner Creator's artistic form. When that happens, life starts to flow with more ease.

Your Inner Pink Star is born from love and holds all your internal creativity and power. She knows every step of the way just how lovable and pure you truly are. She knows immediately what is best for you. She doesn't judge nor put you in harm's way. She is the gateway to happiness, serenity, healing and truth.

Your sense of confusion transitions into a calm, evaluated mindset. She is quiet and often gets overshadowed by your busy mind, the voice of your ego and inner critic. It's time to let your Inner Pink Star guide you through the darkness into the light and straight into your heart, so you can follow the paw prints — those little hints from the universe that your Inner Creator sends you.

It is difficult to quieten our mind and access our Inner Pink Star. Our mind is usually so busy we can't hear through all the chitchat and the grief. To hear her, you need to slow down and be quiet and still. If you practise this, over time she will appear from behind the noise and chaos. Be gentle and give her a chance. If you have ignored her for a long time, it may take a while for her shyness to fall away.

Follow the steps below to call on and connect with your Inner Pink Star. Practise regularly and celebrate when you finally touch your heart; honour her presence and wisdom. Life can change in profound ways when you find your Inner Pink Star, unleash your Inner Creator and follow the paw prints on your heart. Following are the steps to call on your Inner Pink Star.

Calling on Your Inner Pink Star Process

1. Close your eyes and focus on your breath – the inhales and exhales.
2. Be still – Be patient – Be calm – Be silent – Be present.
3. Become the observer; just notice and be aware.
4. Let your thoughts rest and remove any attachment and judgement.
5. Surrender and let go as you go deeper inside.
6. Ask the question that is on your mind.
7. Pay attention and you will find her – the voice of your soul who holds your answers.

Trust the truth of your Inner Pink Star!

Know that your Inner Pink Star always has your best interests at heart; allow her to guide you within and forward through your grief journey.

Pink Pet Love Note

Max, you were my number one main man...

Pink Pet Tools

While I am here to support you, please be honest with yourself as to whether you need immediate professional help. We all need that sometimes. I did too. This book is not a replacement for medical advice. **So please seek professional help immediately if you:**

- 🐾 cannot cope with basic day-to-day tasks
- 🐾 are involving yourself in something illegal
- 🐾 feel triggered by any content in this book
- 🐾 feel like you may harm yourself or someone else
- 🐾 feel your grief is not normal grief. (There are several types of grief that are not covered in this book.)

PART 1

The Loss

My Doggy Life
by Max

"Fairies are animals' guardian angels."

—Doreen Virtue

Here is the love story of two souls connected as one – my mum and me!

I am Max, also known as 'Maxy', 'Mano', 'Maxo the Waxo', 'Maxy the Mano' and Mum's 'main man'. I was given many such silly nicknames during my time on the earthly plane, which may make me seem soppy. I admit that at times I was a little embarrassed. But my human mum gave them to me, so I love them all. I'll actually answer to anything especially if it comes with food or a cuddle!

I'm a golden retriever with a big clown smile. My aim is to please and please some more, but my main purpose is to love my mum unconditionally. As I sit here over the Rainbow Bridge and recall my life, I feel blessed. I had many years of good times and the occasional bad times, full of fun, naughtiness, hilarity, peace, sadness, rest, play, youth, age, health and sickness. But most of all, from day one to my last breath, I had profound unconditional love to give.

Loss, Love and Lessons

Mum taught me that it's important to look back and see how far we have come as it reminds us of what we have achieved and how deeply we love and have been loved. I see my life as a beautiful love story that unfolded over nearly fifteen years and continues despite our two hearts (mine and my mum's) being physically separated. You see, we are still joined at the heart space even though I am over here at Rainbow Bridge.

My life began with a whole bunch of golden siblings and Mum and Dad Dog. Playtime in our pen was fun and natural. We were often busy yelping and biting each other, tossing and tumbling over each other. I don't think Mum and Dad Dog played quite as much. They used this as a time to rest but occasionally they would drop and join us. Other times they would put their paw on our heads to calm us down and remind us to rest. We got a little out of control sometimes, creating golden retriever chaos with fur flying everywhere.

Puppy life was great with no worries or concerns except wondering when Mum Dog would come back to the pen so we could eat again. Life was a balance of playing, resting, eating, sleeping and pooping. If I thought about it, I presume I would have expected my siblings and I to live happily ever after in the same pen at this house where we had entered the world.

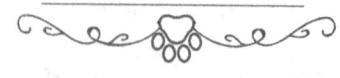

I am here to give unconditional love.

One sunny day after another morning of frolicking in our pen, a young lady entered our space and I instantly felt her presence. Others had come before her, yet there was something different about this one. I could sense she was kind and loving. She radiated a beautiful energy yet there was something lacking inside – a piece of her that needed to be filled. My heart just knew it was meant to join with hers. I could fill that void. Her joyous nature had her swooning over all of us puppies, going from one to the next, cuddling and patting our golden furs.

My Doggy Life by Max

I fell instantaneously in doggy love. This was different to my love for my siblings. I felt an instant bond with this lady, and I needed her to know this. We were meant to be together! Sometimes you just know when you meet your forever person and you need to do whatever it takes to ensure the opportunity doesn't pass you by. But she was so enthralled with us all. How could I get her attention?

I saw my opportunity. I scampered over to the wall where this long piece of wood with prickly bristles on the end was leaning, and I collided with it. It pricked my nose and threw me backwards as I lost my footing. It fell to the ground with a loud noise. She stopped and turned. I had her attention! I looked like an upside-down turtle flailing about. I added a few little squeals and she came straight over to me! She set me onto my feet again and chuckled before she scooped me up into her arms and held me tight.

I was instantly overcome with a sense of warmth, affection and safety. I stopped wriggling and looked straight into her eyes, filling her with all my love. It must have worked because she was captivated. We stood in stillness, just basking in the love flowing between us. Just being present.

"This is the one!" I heard her say to her male friend. "This one with the green ribbon." I wasn't sure exactly what that meant but it felt good. I started wriggling in her arms with joy! But soon after she put me down, patted my furs and left.

I teach you to be present in the moment.

I was distraught.

As I went about my daily doggy duties, I kept thinking about her, wondering and waiting. Finally, a few weeks later as I was scurrying around the pen with my siblings, I felt something different. The energy had changed. I turned around and there she was. My heart stopped for a microsecond and then burst open. She bent down and picked me up again, holding me tight. Again, that sense of warmth and safety engulfed me. Next thing we were off. I was chosen!

I barely had time to farewell my furry siblings or Mum and Dad Dog, which made me a little sad, before I was put into a large vehicle. We headed off on what was to be a lifetime adventure.

This was the start of our love story, and what a beautiful love story it was... and still is.

My home

I arrived at what my new human mum (Mum) said was to be my new home and went about eagerly discovering every inch. I peed on everything possible outdoors to make sure everyone knew this was my house. I felt so proud. In the kitchen, Mum pointed to a big sign and read out the words to me in an excited voice: "Welcome home, Max!" Underneath there was a new cosy bed just for me with a few toys inside. What really caught my eye was a big stuffed toy that looked exactly like me!

I now had a place to call home and it felt wonderful.

Our life was amazing and fun-filled for the first few years. At first, it was about settling into my new home where there were no siblings and no outside pens. I learnt about indoors, warmth and couches. I learnt all about outdoor sprinkler systems and did all I could to assist by chewing through all the sprinkler heads. I was given pink tennis balls and carried them around the backyard, bouncing them off the pavement and finding warm places to sleep with them tucked under my arm.

I tried to make friends. One time I was chasing a bee all over the garden. He was fast, but I was much more skilled on my feet and I got him. Next thing I knew my face became unbearably itchy.

My Doggy Life by Max

I panicked and ran inside at full speed to show Mum, who also instantly panicked at seeing my swelling face.

I could feel my face growing larger with each breath and it was getting a bit hard to breathe. I was put in the car quicker than ever and raced to the vet for a big injection that almost made me faint. But luckily my breathing eased, and we all calmed down. I decided after that to leave the bees to do their thing and instead, I picked flowers and left them for Mum all over the backyard. I liked leaving her gifts as a sign of my love. She didn't always think it was that great as I cleared all her plants.

We went on daily walks together and discovered all the local parks, creeks, shops and streets. I got to smell out all the local animals and take my place in our community. Mum wanted me to learn about my environment and community. She told me this would help me to feel like I fitted in and that I was part of something bigger. It would help me to socialise and provide physical, emotional and mental environment enrichment. By doing this, I was to become a good family pet.

It was a tough few years in some ways as it all seemed to be about the training. I had to sit for everything: before I got in the car, before dinner, before I went through a doorway and before I went outside. Luckily, I didn't have to sit before I pooped. We went to puppy school and training school, and I continued to excel at all my commands especially when there were rewards like chicken and cheese.

I had to drop, wait, give, take, stay, come (that was a hard one as I got distracted – I loved to sniff), shake a paw and roll over. I wondered for a while if I was in a doggy bootcamp or if I was going to be a special show doggy with all my tricks.

I was taught hide and seek and chasey as we ran through the house. So many games and so much fun. Spending all my time with Mum and learning all the tricks was simply good fun! I felt it was all about me and I loved that. Later, I understood that all the training, which was filled with love, was just another one of Mum's ways to make sure I was going to be a good family dog.

This phase of my life grounded me and taught me early that family and our loved ones are everything. Mum taught me that love is the point and that it is as important to give as to receive love, all with an open heart and a big clown smile. I was infatuated with her smile and the way she laughed at all the silly things I did.

You are my home and family.

And that empty space inside her had filled up!

Every day, if I was not with Mum, I laid at the front door or the front gate and just waited for her to return. I was a loyal and devoted friend who just wanted to be with Mum. We dogs wait a lot. We sleep as we wait, but each time our love person arrives home it is worth the wait! I would put on a big show, so she knew how excited I was. I butt wiggled from the gate all the way through the house like I hadn't seen her for weeks.

Life had a smooth and luxurious routine that I sunk easily into. Each night concluded with a big dinner, lots of cuddles and a beautiful sleep in a big, warm doggy bed with my life-sized toy dog and adventurous doggy dreams. Life was pawfect!

And then it wasn't...

I was about two by now and I sensed something different. I still felt the love from my mum, but it was shrouded by something heavier going on in her heart. She didn't seem happy, and I couldn't work out why. We still went walking and our routine was the same, but something was wrong.

I tried even harder to please her but grew a little worried as we dogs can sense all your feelings. When you are unhappy it can make us anxious. We know what is going on most of the time. It just oozes out of you humans in all your complicated emotional vibrations. I would lay my head on her lap and look lovingly into her eyes. That seemed to ease her heart a little – my special love elixir.

Then one day she didn't come home. I was still at the same house with the nice man who also lived there, but she was no longer a daily fixture. Where was she? I was sad, lost and afraid. I would sit outside, upright, at the gate waiting for her to arrive. I would lay on the lawn in the sun, drop, wriggle and roll and dream of our earlier times.

No one played with me as much and I was alone a lot. I was lonely. Had I done something wrong? It was such a confusing time. I pined for Mum each day, hoping she would return and things would go back to normal. Each time the gate opened I hoped it was her. She did occasionally pop in and I perked up as we went for a walk, but they were short and she seemed preoccupied. After she tussled my fur and told me how much she loved me amidst many tears, she would be off again. I just had to ride out these days, thinking it will surely get better.

When we walked, Mum often spoke about how we have times in our life when things are going well and times when they are not. She explained that life can change quickly and it can be very scary when we are thrown into a new routine. Emotions heighten, but then things change again and we come back into balance. "We need to learn to go with the ups and the downs, Max," she'd say. "It's just a part of life, like the seasons. Everything is temporary. This is just a season, Max, so let's ride it out. Things will work out soon."

I trust in the journey.

So, despite my hurting doggy heart, I continued to sit by the front gate, hoping for better days. Days she would be a part of again. I believed her words, "Sometimes it's just about holding on for the ride and trusting in the journey. Better days are coming".

A New Home and Back Again

Mum arrived one day quite chirpy and began collecting my stuff. "Come on, Max, let's go!" What was happening? She kept saying, "Come on, Max!" Where were we going? I followed her around with a skip in my step, hot on her heels, checking she collected everything including the big red Kong toy and the life-sized golden retriever toy that had been sewn up numerous times from my excited chewing. If there were no toys around, I needed to get a shoe. But Mum didn't bring any shoes with us...

After some time and a little bark to signify we had everything, we were all put into the car. We were off on another journey, ears flapping in the wind. I was sure this was the day. After all the days of waiting, this was the start of the better days.

We drove for a short time and ended up at her sister's where I had been numerous times before. It was a house filled with love and children. I always felt happy and safe there, with so much to do and lots of scraps on the floor to eat. All my things got unpacked. I was still a little confused but understood that I must be staying here as my bed was placed in a warm and cosy spot.

I had a short six-month stint there with my extended family, which I enjoyed. Mum would visit often, but I still dreamt of the days where we woke up together and went to bed together at night. Would that ever happen again?

Find the gratitude.

Life was good, but it could have been so much better. I would continue to hope because without hope what have we got? I was very grateful that I had people to love me, a warm bed, lots of food and walks. I was lacking for nothing. Mum often cried for all the doggy souls who didn't have anything and wished she could help. I knew I was one of the lucky ones.

Then one day it happened. Mum's sister called for me in the backyard as I was basking in the sun. "Max, let's go home!" By then I knew what 'home' meant. I hadn't forgotten, and I ran, sliding out on the floorboards to be part of the action. I was still a young pup and a little overexcited at times. In the car I jumped and spied on the back seat a box with all my belongings including my favourite red indestructible Kong and my soft, shabby golden retriever toy.

We pulled up outside a beautiful little cottage, and I was confused for a moment. This didn't look like home. But out walked Mum with a huge smile and the biggest hug! Home was wherever Mum was. I bounded in and could smell her all through the house. I ran from one end to the next as the box with my belongings came through the door, nearly being hurtled to the ceiling as I ran past it. I jumped on her bed and noticed on the floor a giant new doggy bed. It all started to come together. All my toys got spread through the house as I sniffed and inspected. Was this my new home? Then Mum confirmed, "Max, you are home, finally".

That night was the best. All the waiting by the gate and the pondering in the sun had paid off. I was home, and that night we once again fell asleep in the same room together. The doggy bed on the floor was so comfortable, but I decided sleeping on her bed with my head on the spare pillow was definitely a better spot to lay my head. I tried to check that I didn't have muddy paws before I leapt up, got comfy and closed my eyes.

Another routine ensued in discovering a new neighbourhood with daily walks, park visits and creek swimming, visiting friends, going to work at the vets with Mum, drinking coffee at cafes, spending time at the river as Mum waterskied and going to the beach for swims. One time, coming home, Mum sat in the back with me and I vomited all over her. I learnt not to drink the sea water... oops. Then there was visiting Nanna and her friends at the retirement village where I was offered many biscuits and much more fun stuff.

Loss, Love and Lessons

Life was better than fabulous.

I even joined Mum on a houseboat holiday and had to wear a thick jacket all week. They called it a lifejacket. I got to swim all day and hang out by the fire at night. It was cool, fun and nice to be included rather than left at home. Mum made sure I was never left out. When she had to travel for work, she found someone to housesit so I could stay at home in my surroundings rather than going to a kennel. I heard they could be hit and miss with how they looked after you.

I did get into a little altercation with some Weimaraner dogs at the park once and ended up a bit worse off. But I can assure you they started it! Mum was scared but I was tough. I could look after myself. The blood dripping from my face turned out to be only a surface wound.

I had a few operations for various things at the vet and always ended up with a huge bucket on my head. I tried hard turning myself into a pretzel to get around it to lick at my stitches, but it was impossible. I eventually surrendered and just endured the uncomfortableness.

I was growing up day by day. Mum and her friends always said I was turning into a handsome, well-mannered gentleman (with a little bit of cheeky, of course!). The best part every night was when I laid my head on the spare pillow and closed my eyes, but not before pawing Mum's book for more pats before I drifted into sleep. I felt so loved and I gave so much love. I know Mum felt love. I could sense her open and full heart whenever I was nearby, which was most of the time.

Giving and receiving much love.

A FRIEND

Then one day I had to learn one of many life lessons. Sharing!

One of Mum's human sisters had moved in with us a while ago. It was great. I had two lovely ladies fluffing over me. I had no trouble sharing with her! But one day she arrived home with a tiny puppy. It was busy and bitey and small enough to fit in my food bowl. I immediately felt insecure and a little threatened. Hey, this was my house and I was the king of the cottage! I didn't want him eating my Schmackos™!

Mum and her sister, however, made sure we were introduced slowly and appropriately and both given equal attention, which calmed my insecurities. I got to know the little cute dude. His name was Billy and he was a broken coated (partly smooth and partly wiry) Jack Russell terrier. He turned out to be a great mate and no threat at all. I retained my place in the ranks as head dog.

Billy would jump up and hang off my cheek fur, which was a little annoying and hurt a bit. But I tolerated him. I was now a little older and over the crazy puppy days, but he was pretty cute. We would get up to all sorts of mischievousness together as I tried to guide him with his manners and teach him what was right and wrong. But he often led me astray and I mostly didn't argue.

Billy's training went pretty well except for a few occasions. One day, we were at the park and happily exploring. Everything was calm until Billy saw a duck. With one-pointed focus he was gone! He chased the duck down the street at full tilt with Mum's sister following, screaming for him to stop. Of course, Billy didn't listen. Then Mum followed her sister, raising her voice. Billy still didn't listen. Then I was the last in the line, making sure I didn't get left behind and woofing all the way.

Loss, Love and Lessons

We were all running after a duck up the street in the suburbs. It was comical. Billy was having the best time. Me? I'm not so sure. I couldn't run as fast as the little guy and was just relieved there were no cars around. I hadn't yet taught him about roads and cars.

The duck finally few off and everyone came to a sudden halt, almost on top of each other. Billy wondered what all the fuss was about. He was quickly placed back on his lead and finally I could relax. The shenanigans were over.

I had to have a serious woof conversation with him on the way home. "Mate, you could have had us all killed, you know..." and before I could finish my serious spiel, all he said was, "How cool was that? I nearly had him except for those wings!" Then the sister also had a big talk to Billy, who just woofed back, and then she engulfed him in a big hug.

I couldn't allow him to get hurt now that he was my best friend. I never really knew I wanted a doggy best friend until I got one. I had my own friend now. I learnt to share my Schmackos™ and my toys. I loved to play tug and share the bed. I now had a playmate when Mum went out for the day. I never felt alone anymore. He was the best! My treasured friend.

Billy and I would sit together in special sunny spots in the house in silence, coming in and out of napping to bark at a passer-by. We would just enjoy our time together – that is, if Billy could sit still long enough. Nearing the end of the day we would perk up and move ourselves to sit at the front door, looking out the front window, waiting for the mums to come home.

Billy and I had another good friend from around the corner called Murray. We nicknamed him Muzz man or Muzza. He was a little dude like Billy, so I felt that I was their big protector. I always protected my backyard so Billy and Murray would feel safe. One day I could smell danger in the backyard. Something was hiding, but they couldn't fool me, not with my keen sense of smell. I barked my hardest to warn Mum until she finally paid attention. It

My Doggy Life by Max

was a whole rigmarole for her to work out why I was barking, but she found them. A family of big blue tongue lizards was hovering around behind some wooden sleepers. Mum got them out of their hiding place safely and relocated them to the local park. Lizards: 0 – Max: 1!

We were all safe. I had protected my mates and my mum.

Murray would come to visit often, and we were nicknamed 'The Three Musketeers'. We played, we walked together, we ate treats together. We were all young, full of energy and had such fun times, just being dogs together. Our mums enjoyed watching us romp around. I'm sure we filled their hearts with warm, fuzzy feelings of love as we lived and loved life.

I had lots of other friends at the park and many cousins. Spikey and Kaly were two of my favourites. We spent a lot of time in and out of each other's lives. Big families are fun, and friends always boost us up when we feel down. I was lucky I didn't feel down much and had much love around me.

I am filled with both love and sadness as I recall my memories. I would live them all over again if I could. Mum often marvelled at how we dogs could simply be 'present'. She said it's because we have less to worry about. I don't know. I just know I lived in the moment, and my moments with Mum were wonderful.

Friends boost us when we feel down.

A HEALTH SCARE

One day, I was at the vet clinic when, ouch, the vet pricked me with a needle. That hurt! She told Mum she was extracting some cells from a lump about the size of a pimple. After a quick look under the microscope, she came over to us, shaking her head. I heard the word 'cancer'. I didn't understand what it was, but I noted the sombreness in the room and Mum crying.

The next day, I was whisked back to hospital faster than I could process what was happening – with no breakfast mind you – and landed on the operating table. I felt a little dizzy before everything suddenly went blank. When I woke up, which seemed like one minute later, I had a shaved leg, the bucket and stitches. I felt a little sore and woozy. "Just breathe," said Mum's colleagues as they patted me and checked on me. They were familiar, and I felt reassured.

I could sense Mum calming down. She had been almost inconsolable the day before. It was lucky she worked in the veterinary (vet) clinic, so she was able to be with me most of the day. I saw the relief on her face when she was told that they had removed the lump, which was called a mast cell tumour. It was sent off for testing, and meanwhile Mum started to study up on what other nasty surprises could be around the corner for a golden retriever like me.

After three weeks the results came back to show that the cancer was gone. Mum was ecstatic. She was very diligent after that to always check and needle-aspirate any lumps as they arose as she now knew they could be potentially fatal.

Listen to your body.

The week after the surgery I rested a lot – on doctor's orders and Mum's! Every time I tried to do more than I was supposed to, Mum would order me back to my bed, saying, "Max, you need to rest so your body can begin to heal". I did what I was told. Well, I didn't have a problem resting a lot. I'm a dog and that is what we do most of the day anyway.

Besides that incident, I was a pretty healthy dog aside from some hot spots (itchy skin rash) and a little eye operation. I presented twice yearly for my health checks, vaccinations and heartworm injections and took my flea treatments monthly. Mum never forgot. She wanted to make sure I never suffered from any preventable diseases. The needles made me want to faint, but I never argued because the vet also meant treats and more treats. I knew begging for treats always weakened even the strongest humans, especially at the vet clinic where everyone was a pushover for big brown eyes!

Goodbyes and Hellos

Soon after there was a very sad day. All Billy's things were packed up just like mine had been so many years earlier. Billy and the sister left and didn't return that night. I looked everywhere for him, but his things had gone. I followed his smell around the house but could not find him. Tossing and turning all night, my keen senses assured me something had changed.

My friend was gone. Where was he? I had to entertain myself at home during the day with no one to hang out with. Mum took me to work some days but not all the time. I had love surrounding me all the time. I had safety, protection, a warm bed, good food, treats and cuddles. But I missed Billy. He was my wingman!

I learnt I could still see Billy. He still came to visit, and I went to visit him. But he now lived in a different house. It was not the same, but I learnt to adjust to my new life. I had Mum and she had me. It was kind of fun doing things just one on one again.

Mum did a lot for me to not feel so alone. I was often left with a special chew toy, treats to hunt out in the backyard, television for some noise, Kong toys filled with treats and many other ideas. Plus occasionally Mum would surprise me at lunchtime for a quick hello and a ruffle of my furs.

Life continued as two souls connected as one: Mum and me... until...

Many months later, when I was resting quietly in the afternoon sun, Mum arrived home with a small, round, tubby white furball. A crazy eight-week-old golden retriever. She was loud and barky and kept jumping up and hanging off my cheeks just as Billy had done as a little puppy when he could fit in my food bowl.

Even though I still missed Billy's everyday company, I was now too busy with my new friend to fret. I remember thinking, 'Oh dear, here we go again!' I learnt that if I sat tall, she couldn't reach my cheeks and she hung off my chest furs instead. I couldn't quite get her to understand, aside from a few little growls, that she was hurting me. She was a hyperactive white fur ball.

Her name was Suzy, and I learnt over the next few days that she was here to stay. I had to start teaching her everything like I had with Billy, ensuring I spent extra time on barking. But nothing seemed to alleviate her need to voice all her concerns loudly. At least we didn't have any duck incidents. She was always at Mum's feet and mastered the 'come' command instantly.

Suzy would come up to me while I was chewing my favourite toys and just bark in my face. She had a lot to learn in the way of manners. I took the easy road and dropped the toy and just let her have it. This became a habit and I often had to just walk away from her barking and let her have whatever she wanted.

I was pretty easygoing though and happy to oblige. Sometimes it's easier to surrender to the moment and the situation. I was a lover, not a fighter. But I was a protector! I explained to Suzy all about the Weimaraners and my fight. I noticed she had an instant dislike for any she met.

My Doggy Life by Max

I was pleased that Suzy was a girl because finally Mum could buy a pink collar for her and a blue one for me. For years, I had been parading around the suburbs in a pink collar because that is Mum's favourite colour. It was a little hard to assert my manhood all around town dressed like a girl. Finally I felt like a man!

I grew madly in love with Suzy and her loud voice. I just wanted to make her happy and settled. As each day went by, we bonded at a very special deep level. Like two furry peas in a pod, we created fur storms through each room in the house. Then she would curl up next to me and sleep, never wanting to be on her own.

Even the first night she arrived, Suzy was put her on her own bed by Mum. But she came to me on my bed. Mum picked her up and asked Suzy to stay on her own bed. But she came over again. Mum put her back on her bed and so it went on. This happened numerous times over many nights until Mum gave up and just pulled Suzy's and my doggy beds together. I was a little miffed that I was now sleeping on the floor and not on the spare pillow. But Mum explained that the bed wasn't big enough for everyone and Suzy needed me to cuddle up to. Sometimes I snuck up in the middle of the night to be with Mum when Suzy was asleep.

I had a sister. I was no longer alone! But my goodness she kept me busy, and even though I was seven she made me feel like I was about two. She had so much energy and it rubbed off on me. We were inseparable, doing all our daily routines together and both going to work with Mum and hanging out in the vet office. Soon I didn't mind the night cuddles either.

Life was fun and my big clown smile was permanent. Suzy taught me a lot about playing and having fun especially after many months of being on my own without a fur friend. Every night I would lick her head and give her a wet mohawk – a sign of my love. The three of us were a family.

Licks of love!

Our needs

Mum always listened and observed our body language to see what we needed. When we would go for walks, she would remove her shoe and place her bare foot on the ground to check the pavement wasn't too hot. When we went to the beach, we would go early morning to avoid the hot sand. I would run deliriously along the beach trying to catch all the quicker dogs and totally exhaust myself.

Luckily, I loved swimming, so I could cool down in an instant, although I am not sure Mum was too impressed with all the scratch marks she endured as I tried to climb on top of her when my feet couldn't touch the bottom.

Mum would watch our tails and our furs, looking for body language when we met new dogs to make sure we felt comfortable with them. She kept her eye out for unfamiliar things on our walks that we tried to pick up and eat. She checked the weather regularly, leaving the air conditioning on for us if it was too hot and making sure she was home if there was thunder as Suzy was a frightened little girl when the skies growled.

We were walked every day at least once and given time with our park friends so we could run around and burn our energy while socialising. We were fed morning and night around the same time as she knew how important it was for us to have a routine to feel safe.

I thought it was funny that she witnessed most of our business and picked all the poops up while checking if they were healthy. She also made sure before we were locked inside at night that we had done a wee and our nightly poop.

We had many treats but were not overfed as she understood extra weight on dogs can cause extra disease and worsen arthritis. It was a balance. We had dentals when the vet suggested them to

My Doggy Life by Max

keep our teeth and gums clean and healthy. She was a great mum. I suppose with working at the vet clinic, she was highly attuned to what we needed. We were definitely living our best furry lives.

Each Christmas we were dressed up in tinsel, Christmas bandanas or big red ribbons and we would head off to the local park Christmas party. There were always lots of doggy treats and crazy looking dogs with silly outfits. Suzy and I would chuckle to ourselves as we didn't have to wear the full head-to-tail outfits like some smaller ones. That was until they recruited me at the vet clinic to be a furry Christmas elf as dogs came in to be photographed with Santa. I didn't mind the outfits too much, but the tinsel was itchy! The humans liked it though and our job was to please them, so looking like a Christmas tree once a year was something I could bear.

I always felt safe. But more so if I was inside. I had a thing about doors and always pushed through first. But the bigger issue according to Mum was if I was stuck outside when, much to her disgust and embarrassment, I would destroy whatever was in my way to be inside.

Firstly, she had to pay to fix the sister's dog door that I chewed off. That one was tough as I had a bucket on and they found me sitting, looking like a perky frilled-neck lizard with the bucket around the wrong way, after destroying the dog door to get inside.

At the parents' house once, I managed to chew off their dog door but then realised the hole was too small for me to get through. So I just kept chewing frantically around the wood while Suzy barked at me till the neighbours arrived, fearing something was wrong.

I came across a similar situation at another sister's house after I managed to curl into the smallest version of myself to get through her tiny dog door. The door broke but I didn't have to chew it off. Inside once again!

At the boyfriend's house, I chewed through the fly screen door and it got a little stuck as I could not chew through the next glass door. My only failed attempt. Yes, doors were my thing. I was like Harry Houdini backwards: I didn't want to get out but in because that's where all the people were. I needed to get to the front door to wait for Mum. Call me Max, the great escape artist (in reverse)!

> Wait at the gate for the one you love.

I was getting a little bit older when our family grew overnight. All of a sudden Suzy, Mum and I welcomed a male human friend and his two children into our house. It was fun with more people to love, more things to do and places to go. We had a new house to move into, new areas to explore, new parks to visit, new walking trails and new doggy smells to sniff.

We still had prime position in the bedroom on the floor despite Mum having to fight for our spot with her new friend. She won out, which was lucky. But I don't think there was ever a chance of any other alternative. I knew she always put us first. I had learnt that things could change suddenly and to trust that I would always find the best in every situation.

Life went on for some time until I was a little greyer when I sensed that feeling Mum got when she wasn't happy. We had been through this before. Her sadness and a little anger oozed out of her on every dog walk.

I modelled to Suzy that at such times as these, we are just meant to shower more love over Mum, hoping to fill the growing void inside her. I had to draw out my special love elixir and teach Suzy to do the same. We would both put our heads on Mum's lap and look at her lovingly with our sad eyes and console her tears. Things finally got better, and the three of us moved to a beautiful new house. As we settled in, I felt Mum's heart open again and feel loving and happy. It took time though. She explained that at different times in our life we will lose someone we love from a breakup or maybe a death. She talked out loud about grief and the different stages you may go through. I didn't really understand it all, but I just continued to love her and fur up all her outfits as she let my head rest in her lap.

Maybe I took on some of Mum's pain during her breakup because I began to feel a little more exhausted than normal and my legs a little stiffer. I also wanted to sleep more. I would get excited about the park but didn't jump and run around anymore. I just slowly pottered around, seeing what delicious smells I could find. I was getting older.

I would often have to sit down and just take in the breeze through my ears and furs, looking up to the sky and thinking about life while I rested my legs. I couldn't jump into the back of the car anymore. Mum had to lift all 36 kilograms of me into the car and out again, every day.

I wished I could have helped her more, but I just didn't have the strength or the energy. I watched with envy as Suzy still had the vigour of a young adult with health and fitness on her side as she flew up into the car. She still had a long life to lead. It felt good knowing that one day when I was gone Mum would still have Suzy.

Being present

I missed not having the strength and spirit of my youth when I could run all day. I pined for those long beach walks when I could go for hours. But things hurt, and even though we dogs are very good at masking our pain, I knew when I had to slow down.

I tried not to be sad though. I continued to live in the present moment knowing that each moment was a good moment with the three of us. I looked back with joy at my life and I knew that at some stage my health would fail. I was nearly fifteen by this stage and had seen many of my friends disappear from the park at younger ages. I felt like a distinguished gentleman with the golden fur on my face now fading and being replaced by a grey tinge.

ACHES, PAINS AND HOSPITAL

My aches and pains grew by the day and Mum catered for my needs with arthritis injections and special food for my joints. She observed that my gait changed, and she quickly added inflammation tablets to my world to help my pain. I think the tablets made me a bit light-headed and wobbly on my feet some days, or maybe it was just age.

My legs became so stiff that I would slide out on the floorboards and couldn't get up. Once Mum came home to find me stuck and splayed out, and I had pooped myself. It was so humiliating. But Mum to the rescue. The next thing I knew I was wearing little red booties with Velcro® around my ankles. This strange fashion accessory felt weird. They were like little sandshoes that gripped to the floor, so I no longer splayed out and got stuck, and no more embarrassing poo stories. Every morning she would put them on and every night she would take them off. She really thought of everything!

I had a lot of time to do nothing. Sometimes Suzy's loud barking would get to me. Mum encouraged me, saying, "Max, when you love someone, you love all of them – the good and the not so good. You can't change them". So, my love for Suzy won out as always, and I just breathed through it.

One night soon after that, I suddenly had no energy or strength and when I tried to stand up, I fell over. I started kicking and howling, and my body began convulsing. I was foaming at the mouth and lost control of my bodily functions. I also couldn't breathe well! Everything went black then until I found myself at the emergency centre in the middle of the night in a steel cage. 'How did I get here? Where is my warm bed, and why is Mum in her pyjamas?' The nurses said I'd had a seizure. "It was terrifying," said Mum.

I went home the next day and Mum was constantly on the lookout for another seizure. A week later another one arrived. I did feel a little bit strange beforehand, but I didn't know how to communicate this to Mum. It quickly overtook my body, sending it into a seizing mess. I couldn't remember anything and woke up in a strange place, feeling completely drained again.

Then the medications came, trying to balance out the seizures. Mum had a trip planned to Italy with her family, and I spent two weeks at the vet clinic with her friends and colleagues. I could tell she was devastated to leave. "I'm sorry, Max, but this is a once-in-a-lifetime trip with my father to return to our heritage in Italy." I trusted her, as usual, and I still had the familiar faces of the doctors and nurses nearby if I had another violent seizure. Mum hoped that while she was away, they would sort my seizures out with a concoction of medication.

The vet staff plied me with treats and lived up to my every demand. I would walk to reception when I wanted to do my business and the nurse would take me outside. Then I would sit on the grass and not move. I had them fooled. I wanted more outside time, and this is how I took control of the situation. I could tell when the nurse was getting a little flustered with me not moving, and eventually I would give in and return to the clinic. I would begin to feel weary anyway and wanted my bed.

I missed Mum and Suzy so much. I sensed things were not good; maybe the end was near. This was not a quality life for me. For an old dog, or any dog really, it's all about the quality of life. I loved my life and I loved my family, but when you can't do all the wonderful things you want to do, and when it hurts even to cuddle up in your bed and you struggle to do your business without falling over, you begin to lose hope. Throw in no appetite and just feeling lousy and it wasn't a great life anymore.

In my own doggy way, I accepted my reality. Would Mum feel the same?

I soon found out.

One night quite late at the vets, I was still out of my bed in the treatment room and just chilling with the nurses when I felt it. I sensed her energy before she entered the room, just like that first day we had met when I was a pup. It was stronger now though as I had lived my whole life with her. I knew her smell anywhere. Mum was here, finally. My body started to shake uncontrollably, and my heart started beating so fast I almost worried I would make myself sick, poop myself or have another seizure.

The door opened and in she walked, looking a little tired. I wanted to run to her, but my legs let me down. I was stuck to the bed. Everything hurt too much and I felt quite groggy from medication. She ran over and fell to her knees and gave me the biggest hug, stroking my fur and telling me what a good boy I was. I knew she could feel my heart and my shaking and recognised that it was my welcome home to her. She sensed the love.

My belongings were gathered and into the late dark night we went for the short drive home. I was able to sleep on my bed in my room with my mum. Despite the aches and pains, it was beautiful. I could not have been happier, and I had the best sleep ever. Waking to see Mum next to me brought a big clown smile to my face and filled my heart completely.

A LAST DAY

Two days later things took a turn for the worse. I knew it and I think deep down Mum also knew it. The day started with another ferocious seizure. Mum sat with me till I came out of it. It took me a few hours to get over it, despite added medication. So I just laid on my bed. Mum told me to rest and not push my body past its limits. My limits were pretty slim at present and it didn't take me much convincing to rest.

Mum came in loaded up with all her photo albums and sat on my bed with me. For the next few hours, we scoured through them all as she patted my furs, which were a little less silky due to age but furry and full nevertheless. She went through every album, talking to me about our times together, laughing and crying, just soaking up all our beautiful memories from when I was a little puppy full of vigour to becoming old and ill and nearing fifteen.

We were just being together. I remember her saying to me, "Max, you need to give me a sign". I understood what she meant. She wanted me to help her make a decision. I had heard her on the phone to a few people and I could sense a sadness deeper than I had ever felt in her before. It didn't take long for me to realise her sadness was because of me.

I was okay, though – not great but okay. I had come to a sweet acceptance while she was away that my life had been great. Mum and I had lived it to the full every moment. I didn't want to leave her, but my doggy intuition knew that it was time and I accepted it. So, sadly, I now had to live in that particular moment.

I had been lucky. Fifteen is a very good age for a big dog. My quality of life was poor now though. The seizures were not under control despite the medications. Now was the time. I had to prepare my goodbye.

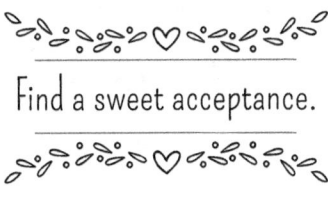

Find a sweet acceptance.

I was ready. You see, I knew that no matter what, we would be together even if not in a physical sense. We were two souls connected as one, and we would always be. How was I to help Mum through this though? I sensed from her deep sadness that she would not quite feel the same, or at least not for some time anyway.

So in the next breath, I raised my paw slowly and placed it on top of the photo album she was holding. She picked it up, rubbed it and put it back on the bed, smiling softly. I once again picked up my paw and placed it on the album, just like I had done for many years as a young pup when she read in bed and I slept on the spare pillow.

This time she stopped and looked at me, deep into my eyes and directly to my heart. She understood that I had offered her a sign and what it was. We were always so connected. Still, all morning Mum vacillated back and forth and making phone calls. She had a tough decision to make. Her sadness permeated the whole house. Suzy was also moping around, almost glued to me. Then I was overcome by another seizure and Mum sat with me as I recovered. I think this cemented her decision; I knew it had for me. I heard her ask the vet over the phone to come over that evening for something called 'euthanasia'.

A LAST PARK VISIT

I was feeling pretty weak after two seizures in one day, but a few hours later Mum found some motivation and bundled me into the car. We were off to the local park for one last time. There she carefully took off my booties as we always did in the park, lifted all my 36 kilograms out of the car and placed me gently on the lawn.

As my paws sank into the soft grass and I felt the cool of the soil, I sunk into a lay-down position and took it all in. I noticed the breeze on my furs and the love that surrounded me. My life flashed before me, filled with green parks, warm beds, loving family, good food, doggy friends, beaches, boundless energy and lots of love. Despite the ups and downs as it flashed past, it all came with such a loving, positive energy. Then I let it rest and came back to the moment – this special last moment with Suzy and my mum at my beautiful park – and I breathed it all in one last time.

I knew I would never see the park again. I knew this was our last time. I had to make the most of every moment. Mum sat with me, her tears constantly flowing. I didn't really understand why she was sad. Didn't we have many things to be happy about? As dogs I know we don't have as evolved emotions as humans, so it is easier for us to just be in the moment and happy. But my heart did feel heavy — a feeling that I hadn't experienced often.

She was deeply sad, coming out of it a little to feed me some Schmackos™ and give me lots of cuddles as she explained that grief is a dichotomy of the pain of the loss amidst the beauty of the love.

Final Words

I just wished she could lift some of her sadness. I didn't want her to remain in sadness. I wanted to convey to her that I was okay, that I knew it was my time, that I was pleased she had picked up the sign I sent her with my paw. That I was pleased she had picked me all those years ago when I concocted the plan to knock over the broom to be noticed. She sensed my confusion.

She tried to explain to me as we sat on the grass, and this is what she said:

> "Max, grief is about love. Love is about grief. To allow yourself to love allows grief in. To avoid grief you would need to avoid love. My deep grief will be a testament to how much I love you. I will miss you and everything about you. Letting you go will tear my heart to pieces and will be the hardest thing I have ever had to do. To make the decision to end your pain is heartbreaking and will plunge me into the depths of my grief. It will be my final act of love to you. I don't want to hold you here any longer in a body that doesn't function, causing you ongoing daily pain.
>
> "I do not want you to suffer anymore. I know the time is now. Your sign showed me that you know your time is now. I don't want to feel guilt although I might, as this is an act of love, not betrayal. You are my baby boy and I need

to somehow say goodbye. Not to our love but to our daily hangouts, to your physical presence in my life.

"When the time arrives, Max, you will see a beautiful rainbow appear full of colour and life, and I want you to run towards it. You may feel my sadness lingering, but know this is now your new journey that promises you a life free of your daily pain, full of renewed vigour. Your health will be fully restored, enabling you to run and play at your new home called Rainbow Bridge.

"For me, I will be sad for a while, maybe a long while. I will walk to the epicentre of my pain where it is scorching hot and comprises only of tears and deep hurt. Then one day, the days will start to slowly appear brighter and I will ease back to my reality. You will no longer be by my side, but you will be forever scattered in the form of paw prints through my heart.

"I could not love you any more, Max. I thank you for everything. You taught me so much: lessons galore. Especially how to fully embrace and love unconditionally. I will miss you so much until we meet again one day... and we will. I don't want you to sit and wait at the gate though. Enjoy and when I arrive, I will come and find you. Until then we will always be two souls connected as one, holding a love that never dies."

The whole point is love.

Her heart was talking directly to mine, and I sensed and understood exactly what she was trying to say: *The whole point is love!*

I had a few things to say also, which was difficult in dog language. To her it sounded like 'woof woof', but to me it went something like this:

"Mum, you have been the best mum ever and always catered for my every need. Thank you for everything and for teaching me to be a good dog. I could not have wanted for more. I know you are struggling with your decision even though you know it is the right time. It is such an act of love towards me for you to make this decision and plunge yourself into grief.

"But, Mum, I am okay. I am ready to go. I am thankful that you are able to make this difficult decision, but please release any guilt. I don't want to live any longer in this pain. It is no life for me. I look forward to being out of pain, and I will always be in your heart.

"Please don't grieve for too long. Move through your grief with an open heart, and as you remember me and our time together, open your heart to many more beautiful furry souls that need a loving home like you have given me. Visit the dog park with Suzy and enjoy every moment. Live your life as rich and full as you can.

"Be fabulous and live an amazing life. Immerse yourself in life. I love you more than words can say. Thank you for picking me. Thank you for picking the green ribbon – your least favourite colour. Thank you for everything. I will miss you. I love you. Shine your bright light to the world as you cherish our memories and always follow my paw prints scattered all over your heart. They will always remain.

"I came here to this physical world with one purpose and that was to love you unconditionally, and in turn teach you to do the same. I feel I have truly fulfilled that purpose. My life has been full, so I feel I can now transition onwards, always knowing I did what I came here to do.

"It was always you. I am because of you. Two souls connected as one."

Our deep words had been said. Mum could tell my energy was wavering, so she gently lifted me back into the car for my last car ride. She left the window down so I could feel the wind pass through my ears. I always loved car rides and this one was especially special.

A Feast and a Last Goodbye

When we arrived home, I suffered another seizure. We both agreed with a long look that it was time. Amidst the tears, Mum wanted to make the most of the little time we had left. She tried so hard to be chirpy despite her heavy heart.

Mum had always promised me cupcakes for my fifteenth birthday, and it was only three weeks away. But sadly I would never get to taste her doggy cakes. Instead, while we waited for the vet we had a bit of a feast. I got vegemite toast – my favourite – ice cream and doggy chocolate chip cookies.

Mum brushed me till I was all nice and silky smooth. She cleaned my eyes and took off my booties, letting my paws breath. Then with a lot of tears she took off my collar and gently tied a beautiful red bandana with white spots around my neck. It felt strange without my collar, but she placed it nearby.

Suzy helped by licking my head from ear to ear, giving me a big wet mohawk – a trait I had taught her when she was younger in our nightly ritual over many years. I looked slick as I prepared for my passing moment and my upcoming journey. I perked up a little as this was all happening but not too much. I didn't want Mum to renege on her decision. She was doing the right thing by me; this was what I wanted. I didn't want her to feel any guilt. We had to proceed forward despite the pain we were all experiencing.

Not long after our little food feast I heard the door. The vet had arrived. Mum was agitated and teary as they chatted a little before they both came to sit with me. I was calm but a little nervous. I was okay with the decision, but would it hurt? What would happen? Would Mum be there? I wanted Mum right there with me. Most of all I didn't want to feel alone.

My Doggy Life by Max

It all happened rather fast after this. The vet explained to Mum that he would place a tourniquet on my front arm to find a vein and then insert a catheter. He would inject the lethal solution directly into the catheter rather than directly into the vein as this would ensure I would feel no pain. It would work almost immediately. I also heard him say that I would feel like I was just going to sleep. I was pleased that there was going to be no pain.

Suzy was sitting nearby, nearly on my head.

Mum was hugging me tight.

The vet was holding the catheter.

I love you.

Then Mum spoke. "Max, I love you with all my heart. Thank you for everything. I will miss you so much." Then her words turned into sobs. I tried to answer but nothing came out. She knew how much I loved her though.

Next, I heard the vet ask Mum, "Are you ready?" She was hugging me so tight, twirling my ears.

I could feel her soft kisses raining down all over my head as she answered "Yes" ever so softly. The next moment, my eyes slowly and gently closed as I thought, 'I love you, Mum. Please don't feel guilty. Don't be sad for too long. Be happy and remember all our memories. Feel the love I have left in the form of my paw prints on your heart.' I dozed off one last time to the longest and deepest sleep.

A Rainbow

That's the last thing I remember before the spectacular rainbow appeared just as Mum had promised. Its array of beautiful colours caused my heart to overflow. I could feel that each colour was laced with her love despite her looming distance.

I could hear her crying as I transitioned over. I wanted to turn around and run back, but I had always obeyed her and could not let her down at this special time. I could also sense a love coming from over the rainbow that was even stronger than Mum's, drawing me forward! So I followed the rainbow just as Mum had instructed on my journey to my next adventure, feeling safe and protected by her love.

I continued to sense her profound sorrow and sadness as I moved forward. I mustered up all the energy I could to send her my love and light and placed one paw in front of the other as I walked to the rainbow and merged into its illuminous beauty and brightness.

I knew with all my heart that we would meet again when the time was right. We would be reunited one day. But until that special day I sensed I had important things to do and good friends to meet that had long since left on this same path. I hoped they would guide me towards the peace, vitality and health Mum had promised me. Then, in time, I could become a safe paw to hold for other furry friends as they arrived.

More so, though, I hoped my mum would follow the path of her own grief and follow my paw prints on her heart that would walk her to the profound love that awaits her on the other side of her grief journey. I hoped she would openly welcome many more furry souls into her life and offer them what she gave me. I hope she learnt to live with the unconditional love I had taught her, and

My Doggy Life by Max

I hope she always remains in touch with the inner knowing that we are always two souls connected as one, holding a love that never dies.

I will be always watching and ready for her at the gate when she arrives!

Max

Xx

 Losing Max

"He might only be here for a part of your life but for him, you are his whole life."

—Unknown

I begin near the end while I now acknowledge the end as a new beginning.

Looking back, it was a whirlwind month leading up to Max and I saying goodbye to each other. It included one of my biggest highs and one of my biggest lows. I had no clue how this month would change my life forever or even that it was coming. I was so not prepared for what was to follow or how difficult the journey through pet grief would be for me, despite working in the vet industry for well over a decade and being exposed to its sorrows every day.

Max was my first dog aside from my family dogs. He was my fur child, my golden fur angel, my furry guru and my canine soulmate. I would have done anything for him... and did. No time or expense was spared for him to have the very best doggy life.

I met him at six weeks old and brought him home two weeks later. We lived through a full life of ups and downs with him right by my side no matter what. We adored and loved each other unconditionally. Our life together was simply awesome. Friends and partners came and went while Max and I remained inseparable: him always faithfully by my side and me always covered with a layer of golden fur. We were and still are two souls connected as one.

Two souls connected as one.

When I reluctantly left Max behind at the emergency vet clinic after his first seizure, I hoped it was a one-off. Over the next week, while I busied myself with the preparations for a trip to Italy with my father to visit his homeland, thankfully Max appeared to be stable. Then, as you read, two nights before we left, it all changed again suddenly. He suffered another grand mal seizure. Viewing him afterwards in a cage at the vets once again, I was heartbroken and beside myself. I considered not leaving on our trip, but thankfully I arranged for Max to stay at the vet clinic. This soothed me a little as all the staff were my colleagues and friends who loved Max, and he was used to being there most days, just sitting in my office.

He would be in good hands, actually the best. Working at the vet clinic luckily allowed me this luxury of having high-level overnight care by experienced vets and nurses while I was away. My colleagues and friends would care for him while also working on finding the right balance of medications to control his seizures. I presumed they would. I left a massive list of instructions for all the nurses to keep him comfortable.

Departing on the plane was beyond difficult. I was beaming with excitement for our long-awaited trip while deeply worried about leaving Max. My heart was breaking. He had always been there for me and now, in his real time of need, I felt I had deserted him.

While I was away, I received lots of messages from him (well, from the vet staff) and pictures of him. Apparently, he roamed around like he owned the place. He had always been a big, confident, loving dog full of bravado and a little bossy. His confidence was outrageously healthy, and there were still remnants of this even as an ill senior dog.

While travelling around Italy, I struggled to keep myself together, not think the worst and enjoy the holiday. But he was never out of my mind. I occasionally snuck away to the toilets to release another build-up of tears. I feel I compartmentalised my life well for the three weeks I was away and tried to live in the moment to enjoy the trip – a trait I learnt from Max. Dogs are perfect at living in each moment as they arise. They are gifted as our best teachers in this and many other areas of life. I enjoyed the times with family on this once-in-a-lifetime holiday with my father who was also on his own timeframe. Though we just did not know it yet.

After a great trip we finally touched down and I arrived home to an empty house late on a Friday night. I was jet-lagged and tired and should not have driven. But I couldn't deny my strong urge to go and collect Max regardless.

It is always important to listen to our gut feelings and those instinctual pulls. They come from a place inside of us that is full of inner wisdom and knowing. I had learnt this over and over, and so I followed its advice. I couldn't trust my scattered jet-lagged mind anyway. When I arrived at the hospital at about 11pm I found he was not in a good way. He didn't move off his mat, but when his eyes homed in on me, his whole body started shaking and trembling in excitement. I raced to sit and cuddle him, placing my hand on his pounding heart, which seemed to almost burst out of his chest. He was more than thrilled to see me. There were many tears. Mine. We were reunited for now.

I learnt they had tried to balance his medications and his seizures, but his health was still in a precarious position and things were not as good as I had hoped.

The next day we had a lovely relaxing Saturday. We collected Suzy from a friend who was looking after her and we all just hung out, reuniting. Sadly, on the Sunday Max had two seizures before lunch. Seeing him suffer through the seizures, taking hours to recover after and knowing that a month of readjusting meds didn't seem to be helping was heartbreaking.

After lunch that day I had another inner feeling that things were not good. I started to ponder the dreaded decision of euthanasia. He even needed help to toilet by this stage as his back legs wouldn't hold him. Not really knowing what to do with myself, this is when I sat with him and all our photo albums. I hoped the answer would come.

Look to your heart.

Having a sinking sensation that it may be our last day together, yet not able to fully acknowledge it, we went to the park. As his paws touched the grass his spirits lifted slightly, just enough to do his standard drop to the ground, back wriggle with his legs in the air flailing about and lastly rolling over to rest. He then rose to have a little wander before just sitting to take it all in, possibly for the last time.

Losing Max

It was mid-afternoon when the final decision arrived and settled on my heart. It was not a rational, well-thought-out process. More of a feeling. He could not continue like this. Two seizures in one day was too much. I knew things would not improve.

I thought back to earlier that day as we sat looking at the photos and I had pleaded for a sign. This is when Max placed his paw on the albums. This was my sign and it now was time to honour it. He was asking me to help him. His quality of life was no longer good. He had waited patiently for me to return from overseas, suffering with seizures. But he was now asking me to let him go. He was asking for me to follow the paw prints on my heart. I had always promised that I would be by his side when he left this earthly plane.

I was lucky enough that the owner of the vet clinic – also a good friend – could come to my house on a Sunday night to perform a home euthanasia. The vet reassured me that I was making the right decision and that we had done everything we could. Max's final seizure before the vet's arrival cemented my tearful decision. I had no second thoughts. Max was struggling and obviously calling out for help to pass over. I would have done absolutely anything for him, but now what was needed was for me to put him at eternal rest and peace while I would plummet straight into my own darkness.

A little bit of lightness brightened the room for a moment, though, seeing Max lifting his head, eager to take some food. A moment to be grateful for as the darkness loomed. We took some great photos despite my eyes looking red and puffy from a full day of tears. I sat with him and hugged him, spoke to him, patted him and tried to soak up all his energy and love for all the times he would no longer be by my side.

After our food party, I slowly removed his collar and brushed him till his golden fur was soft, smooth and glowing. I placed a red and white spotted bandana around his neck. The animals at the vet clinic receive one of these after surgery; they are called bravery bandanas. Max was one of the bravest dogs I have met. He looked so distinguished and handsome in his bandana, and he needed to be brave for his next journey. I took off his booties so he could feel the air flow through his paws. I fully immersed myself in each touch of his fur and the feel of his beating heart. He was perfect!

I continued to struggle, desperately trying to come to terms with what was to happen later that night, despite knowing I had made the right decision. My love for him had guided me straight to this decision, and to let him go. My final act of deep love for my Max. It was more important to let him go peacefully and with dignity than to keep him in pain to satisfy my own desires. Yet, this pure love tore my heart apart. My anxiety levels had been skyrocketing all day. It all felt so surreal.

Pet grief is made harder because we are the ones making the decisions around keeping them alive or letting them go peacefully to remove their pain. Depending on your perspective and situation, this can propel you directly into intense guilt. I have always said that you will know when the time is right if you look to your heart. To make this kind of decision, though, you need every ounce of inner strength as you know that in removing their pain you are left in your own deepest and darkest pain. This is Love!

So that is what I did. I looked to the love as the vet and the moment arrived. I had to proceed somehow. To add to the heartbreak, Suzy must have known something big was transpiring as she came over and wedged herself between

Max with his glorious mohawk and me, almost sitting on top of him.

I continued to sit beside Max while the vet prepared for the euthanasia. I knew the drugs would act instantaneously and that it would be painless and peaceful as he closed his eyes for the last time. Knowing this didn't really help me though. When asked if I was ready, my whole body was screaming "No!" Of course I wasn't. But from the depth of my heart, the strength and the love mouthed audibly "Yes" anyway.

I had waited all day. A tortuous day that was filled with so much love and recollections. I had to now go through with the moment I had dreaded since the day I brought him home as a puppy, fourteen years ago. I kissed him, twirled his ears, buried my head deep into his fur, put my arms around his neck, and told him how good and loved he was. The next thing I heard was the vet saying, "He is sleeping now. He is gone".

As I lifted my head, I looked outside and the rain was coming down in droves. Buckets of tears from heaven that were all mine while Max's spirit left his body to move to a spiritual realm. There, he would forever rest in the arms of his angels. I prayed he would find his way to the beautiful rainbow that paved the way to his next journey.

I couldn't speak. I couldn't stand, collapsing into my friend's arms. What an unbearable feeling. The grief was agonising. I think my whole body was in shock. Slowly, when I regained some type of composure, we wrapped him in a rug before placing him into the back of the car to take him to the vet clinic where we would arrange his cremation.

Soon after we placed him in the car, Suzy jumped into the back and landed on top of him. She was not letting us take him without her. She looked confused. I put her in the back seat. I could not leave her behind.

From my experience, I believe that it's important for pets to be included in this process and to see the body. Animals understand death, just like they understand birth and how to be a good mother, purely by instinct. Dogs are very intuitive, not only to our feelings but to their environment and other sibling pets.

Sitting on the floor of the familiar treatment room at my work, I looked down at Max who lay still and lifeless with his eyes closed and no rising and falling of his chest as I had watched so many times. No heart beating under his skin that I had felt all morning while he lay still but only asleep. He looked peaceful and no longer filled with pain. There was no physical life left yet he still felt so full of love.

My heart spilled once again as I looked around and the room looked unfamiliarly cold and desolate. I wanted to run but could not bring myself to leave, not while Max was lying next to me. How would I ever leave him alone and cold in this place? I had to sit in my anxiousness and sadness while I worked out how to say a final goodbye and leave.

When I felt ready, we took some paw prints, cut some fur pieces and tied them in a silky golden bow. I chose a cremation urn, and many tears later I said, "Max, I love you and thank you". I squeezed his paws, kissed him and stood on shaky legs. Suzy led me and somehow my legs took me to the car outside. I desperately wanted to run back inside for one more hug. One more goodbye. I felt torn in two. I couldn't go back in though. I knew if I did, I would possibly never leave.

So, I walked onward, feeling suddenly alone and empty as I was launched into the misunderstood world of pet grief.

Max, I love you.

Within a month I was in a place full of grief yet surprisingly packed full of love. The love makes the grief seemingly intolerable, yet the grief makes the love obvious and worthwhile. Paw prints had been left all over my heart by Max, and I had to follow them to heal my grief. And that is what I did. This simultaneously awoke something in me to want to help others like you do the same.

We know dogs generally don't outlive us, and we enter that sacred knowing when the puppy eyes pierce our heart and we fall desperately in love on day one. This love is carried to the end of our time together and beyond. We will meet again, one day. Until then I hope Max doesn't wait at the gate and that he drops, wriggles and rolls at Rainbow Bridge, living his best afterlife while waiting for me just as I wait for him. It's a long time away, I hope! For obvious reasons.

The love I hold for Max is as strong today as it was the day that he left me, maybe even stronger. You see, love is the point. I discovered this again strongly after losing my father. So, I lead a rich and full life in honour of them both, and I strive to live each moment filled with love. I relish the lessons and wisdom Max was sent to gift me, which I share later in this book. He really was my little furry guru!

I love you, Max, my miracle, my guru, my diamond. Please always shine your golden light my way and continue to always be my fur angel from above. Rest in the arms of your angels, play and enjoy life in the evergreen luscious fields at Rainbow Bridge.

Pink Pet Love Note

You were sitting up, still in my arms and looking deep into my eyes. The moment was perfect. I told you I love you. I said thank you and kissed you. I twirled your ears, smelled you, checked your teeth, snipped some furs, took off your boots, removed your collar, ran my fingers through your fur, squeezed your paws, kissed you and locked every part of you in my memory bank, and I waited...

The Path of Grief

"Grief is the price we pay for love."

—Queen Elizabeth II

G rief can be described as an intense sorrow following a loss. Grief and loss rob you of your vital energy and life force. But, believe me, following its path ultimately provides a divinely intended gift: your beautiful heart full of pure love. To find this you need to follow the paw prints scattered over your heart that will lead you all the way to the deep, pure love within you at the end of your grief journey.

It is truly one day and one moment at a time moving through pet grief. Each time you reach down and your friend is not at your feet, or you open the front door and no one runs to greet you, you are reminded once again of the emptiness within you. This void, however, does not need to remain forever. It can be filled up in time if you invest your energy and intention into healing.

Unfortunately, the only way on this journey to get to the place of ultimate healing is straight through the middle of the grief. You must walk to the epicentre where the pain is raw and grates on your soul. The pain from your heart wound commands your attention to feel each emotion, inviting you to analyse less and feel more, to cross over all the rugged terrain until it gradually begins to subside and you find some small reprieves.

This road is full of peaks and troughs. Some days it is excruciatingly painful and all you can do is make it through the day and a river of tears. Other days you feel numbed out, your body protecting you from your deep emotions. Other days you hold anger for the whole world. Maybe sometimes you remember the good times and feel the love. Then this can suddenly remind you again of your grief and you are thrown straight back into the grief cycle.

You may suffer other signs like lack of sleep, digestive issues, fatigue, sore muscles, irritability, loss of appetite or many other physical, mental, emotional, social, spiritual and psychological issues related to your grief. These signs are all a normal part of the grief cycle. Grief emotions may be triggered when something reminds you of them: their favourite toy under the couch or the usual afternoon walk time approaching.

The grief path can move from the initial phase of shock through varying stages including tearfulness, denial, questioning, reality, worry, loneliness, guilt, anger, depression, helplessness, sadness, bitterness, uncertainty and hope to a regeneration of yourself and your life. It does not take a linear path and you can be thrown back and forth between the different phases of grief, at times like a rollercoaster. Unfortunately, it is just a matter of being with whatever grief presents in the moment.

You may want to run and hide from the monster emotions that rise to greet you and threaten to sweep you away. Perhaps uncomfortable and unfamiliar, these emotions may have been hovering under the surface for a long time and this traumatic event has ignited them. Running may seem an easier option than dealing with them. For now it may be. But to heal the grief, to open your heart and return to the love, you must heal the gaping wounds first. That is only possible through feeling your emotions and listening to your grief. I hope you will soon realise this and trust that the only way is forward through this pain.

The Path of Grief

The paw prints pave the beautiful path forward if you place your trust and faith in your inner wisdom, your mutual love with your pet and your inner strength. By surrendering to the journey with self-awareness, you are taking the first steps to your healing.

Take one day and one moment at a time.

Tears may lodge in your throat before they spill over your cheeks. It is these tears of love and grief that help to heal your heart. Try to never suppress them. Allow them to flow. Regrettably, there is no grief map to follow, but once the first step is taken, the rest of the path generally unfolds in front of you with perfect timing. One paw print will lead to the next, which leads to the next. Each moment you are connecting to your grieving heart you are allowing it the space to heal.

If the grief journey is given your love, respect and energy you can, in time, heal. You will still carry grief in your heart; it remains there forever. But it will be assimilated into your life and your heart, with its pain lessening. Grief is about healing the loss, feeling the love and appreciating the lessons.

Grief and loss do change you. Be prepared to notice the subtle inner shifts and know that the changes will eventually settle in your heart and mind, becoming a part of you and your journey. Grief is a major precursor for change. Sometimes these are big, profound changes that are mostly for the better if you are prepared to listen to your grief and follow the paw prints that lead to healing and love, instead of choosing to run and avoid the pain.

Making the commitment to grief is making the commitment to heal. Making the commitment to heal is making a commitment to love, knowing your heart will open and be full of love once again, to share with other humans and more fur children.

Pink Pet Love Note

I feel like my heart has been shattered into a million pieces and you took a piece of it with you. Keep it close under all your fur and know that the love I have for you runs forever, deeply, despite our distance...

Listening to grief

"Dogs have a way of finding the people who need them and filling an emptiness we didn't even know we had."

—Thom Jones

Grief talks to you! It speaks a foreign emotional language.

Your heart is hurting and as you try to make sense of your feelings and emotions, your physical body may be aching and in pain, possibly more pronounced around the heart or gut region. Your whole being is connected, so don't be surprised if you feel pain in various places.

It's likely that you will want to move away from the pain and back to pleasure at any cost. But I propose that instead you accept and experience the grief that will then flow through you, thrusting itself outwards The grief journey does what it needs to do if you allow it and don't force anything. Feel it and be easeful with it. Invite and welcome it in.

Permit your grief to have a voice and listen. Its voice is your rising emotions. At any time you feel the emotions of grief arise – sadness, feeling bereft, depression, anger, fear or any of the whole

The Path of Grief

host of others – acknowledge them and begin to breathe through and into them while you allow their energy to move through you. (We will go into more details on how to achieve this in *Love and Grief Tools and Strategies*.)

As the thoughts arise, allow them to just be in your mind while you practise non-judgement and non-attachment. Try not to follow the thoughts down the rabbit hole. Instead, come back to just noticing the breath. You will clear one emotion and soon the next one will arrive to be dealt with. Practise, repeat and continue.

As the physical body sends you sensations of pain, just allow it to be. Honour it, treat the body gently and listen to the messages it sends to you, such as when it may need to rest, eat or cry.

Invite, surrender, feel and breathe.

It is okay to cry for hours; each tear is a small sign of love and healing. Each falling tear is a doggy lick on your face sent from your pet to help you process your grief and return to a loving, joyful and rich life. They knew how to live in the moment and just be with life, and they are now sending their wisdom to you. They hope you are listening to their cues and continuing on the paw print path.

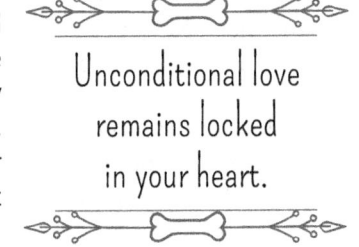

Unconditional love remains locked in your heart.

Sometimes the paw prints are muddy, wet and heavy, walking through your heart-house and staining and ruining your inner carpets, so obvious in their presence. Other paw prints are light and subtle, and you have to pay a little closer attention to find the gift and the wisdom your pet is leaving behind for you.

Being surrounded by others at this time can highlight the disconnection you feel to yourself, your pet, your grief and your life. The numbness and emptiness bring a type of disassociation that separates you from others. You may reach for help but, despite others' good wishes, you will likely feel no better. It's as if a veil has fallen between you and life and you can't find your way around or through it. The world has lost its colour.

You can distance yourself to feel peace and yet only feel more alone. It just all feels strange and frightening, and you might feel befuddled. This is all a normal part of the grief journey. Allow it in and permit your grief to have a voice.

Your body knows the emotions it carries, and it wants to be released from their vice. It spills them up and out, hoping you don't block the process on the way. As the emotions are cleared so is a little of the grief, cleansing your heart and making space for all the love to flow in and bring about profound transformation. Without feeling the not so good we cannot feel the good. Allow the clearing and cleansing to take place.

Trust. Have faith. Surrender! I promise you that the voice of grief will eventually change its tune. But first, you must give yourself permission to grieve. Doing so makes the process more therapeutic and possibly prevents you moving to a more complicated grief that is difficult to heal and more destructive to your fragile heart.

Giving yourself permission puts you actively on the grief journey. You are surrendering and accepting that for now, or for however long it takes, this is your journey. You take responsibility and make a choice, and from it comes a willingness deep inside to take the path to inward healing. A call to the universe is placed to provide what you need, with the promise that you will ride the waves presented to you. There will be many.

It takes courage, self-love and commitment to accept this path. But be assured that it will ultimately bring the rewards, gifts and lessons of love, and a deep connection to self and others. The grief path opens to you a space to heal and an inner awareness of what your heart and soul need right now. It is a reverent sign of honour, self-love and respect to yourself to state this permission out loud.

The Path of Grief

Your heart most likely feels aching and tender as if it needs to be wrapped up in a nice warm, fluffy rug and put to bed to be nurtured through grief. Give yourself this gift. Be kind and loving to yourself just like you were to your pet when you helped them pass over. The paw prints on your heart are your pet giving back to you for all that you did for them. It's now your turn to be cared for!

I know it hurts so much; of course it does. It can be totally unbearable. When the bond seems to be broken through our pet's passing, the deep grief can come as a surprise. Not everyone will understand...

Pink Pet Love Note

Max, I trusted my inner wisdom, accepted your sign and surrendered to my heart to find the decision I needed to make. As I accessed the love, it came to me that I had to peacefully allow you to go, to remove you from your pain with love, dignity and grace...

Societal Conditioning

"The one best place to bury a good dog is in the heart of his master."

—Ben Hur Lampman

In general, people are uncomfortable with grief. It is just the way our society is. To make it worse, society does not strongly validate or support pet grief. This can leave the grieving individual embarrassed and fearful of reaching out, feeling their grief will be viewed as unwarranted. This is so far from the truth. It is important that you understand and accept that your grief is indeed worthy and very real.

The topic of grief, emotions and the ending of life is simply difficult. People often do not know what to say or how to handle the situation or the emotions that arise in you or them, when presented with your grief and cry for support. You will hear things like, "It was just a pet," or "You can get another one," or "You know they don't live very long". Or even, "It's about time you move on from your grief and get on with life". These all amplify the difficulties around pet grief and the attached stigma.

Conversations around grief possibly highlight people's fears around mortality and they may prefer to avoid the discussion. Generally, people are uncomfortable around strong emotions because it may highlight or even bring to the surface emotions they have been suppressing. When people are skilfully living in avoidance, suppressing and repressing emotions, it doesn't take much for these feelings to spill into their conscious mind. There is nothing like grief in someone else to do this.

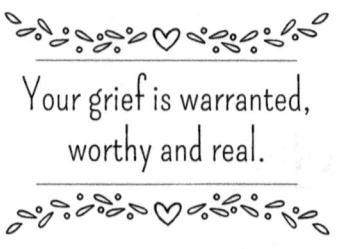
Your grief is warranted, worthy and real.

People tend to move away from pain and towards pleasure. While good in theory, if there is enormous pain just below the surface, to move towards the true pleasure and access it you will have to firstly walk through the pain and heal it. Once you have done this, the pleasure you find below it is true and pure. It's joyful and content.

The pleasure a lot of people look for today is the distraction of instant gratification and excitement – a new car or a new skirt – that simply pushes down unacknowledged feelings of unworthiness or unhappiness. But what goes up must come down. It may be wiser to strive to be like the yogis whose aim is to live in a state of flow, balancing out their emotions to prevent the extremes of high

The Path of Grief

and low that bring unhappiness and emotions that take over the psyche. They choose instead to experience and breathe through each situation.

You may also encounter anticipatory grief, a grief that occurs before death, which is common for those who are facing an impending loss. You may feel the love of your pet beside you and in the same breath feel sadness and pain, knowing they will not be with you much longer. It is easy to vacillate between emotions at this phase of your pet's life. This stage sees us striving to find a balance between holding on and letting go and can bring out many deep emotions involving anger and loss of emotional control. It is not often discussed and, again, others often find it socially unacceptable so we often don't express the pain we are experiencing in fear of what others may think. Anticipatory grief does not replace grief after death, but it can provide an opportunity to help find some closure and provide a chance to say goodbye.

Everyone has had different experiences with life, loss and grief. We are all sitting in different states of emotional unrest, and these are precursors to how others will deal with your grief. It is not about you and mostly about them.

No doubt they always mean well, but that does not stop them from sounding clueless when the words are spoken. Often people don't know what to say, and to fill the silence something unhelpful comes out rather than just quietly being there for support. Good intentions get scrambled internally by perception, experiences, upbringing, culture, conditioning and uncomfortable emotions. They propel outwards in words that hurt not heal, that alienate and separate, instead of creating connection and support.

It takes someone who is emotionally wise and comfortable in their own skin and grief to sit with others' grief, and the discomfort it can bring, and be helpful. To listen actively and bring true support without offering meaningless, or well-meaning but offending, comments takes real skill. To be able to care for your own emotions while supporting someone who is grieving takes a high emotional intelligence, solid self-love, and a deep understanding of grief and life.

That's one reason why this loss can be a good time to seek out a support network. Investigate carefully and choose wisely, whether it be a friend or a therapist. Be selective with the people you share parts of your story with. Don't place high expectations on others only to be disappointed. Be realistic. Begin to build your own self-love so you can ultimately support yourself more instead of continually needing to reach out or distract yourself with each arising emotion.

Once you find your own self-love you will be happier to sit with your grief. You will shrug off others' unhelpful comments like water off a duck's back without getting angry or agitated. You will understand that their comments are not about you but about where they are at and how they are feeling.

You will be able to be comfortable with your grief and know it is warranted no matter how long the process takes or how many tears you shed. You will know the grief for your pet is as acceptable as any grief, and you honour it accordingly. As you begin to honour yourself, you honour your pet, your grief and your loss with commitment and devotion.

Pink Pet Love Note

Max, I wish I had the power to fix this for you, but I'm immobilised by sadness. I must have faith in the universe, surrender and trust in the process…

Links to Life Events

"... when they go from us, these quiet friends ... carry away with them so many years of our own lives."

—John Galsworthy

Often our pets are linked to other events in our lives that add to our grief when we lose them. It can complicate the grief and make it more of a struggle to muddle through.

- 🐾 The animal might have been a deceased parent's pet and were the last link to them. You feel like you are grieving your parent's death all over again.

- 🐾 Your parent may have entrusted you with the care of their pet on their deathbed and now you have had to make the decision of euthanasia and feel horrendous guilt.

- 🐾 Perhaps your child has had the pet since they were born. So besides consoling your child, you feel like you are losing a part of their childhood and innocence.

- 🐾 Maybe losing your dog highlights that ten or fifteen years have passed just like that. One minute they were a puppy running around crazily and the next they were a grey-haired and slow senior. You are reminded of your own age and mortality. Life is passing by. Many older people avoid getting another dog as they fear the dog will outlive them, so they are left alone with no companion.

- 🐾 Or life has been cruel in taking your young pet from you far too soon. The one soul you could rely on for unconditional love is gone. Your heart is broken and you feel ripped off.

- It could be that by allowing yourself to feel the grief of this loss all the other losses that may not have been processed arrive to be dealt with too. This is called transference and can propel you further into the grief cycle. You muddle through and try to separate out what is related to your pet and what is related to another incident from possibly years prior. It's a whirlpool.

There are so many reasons why pet grief hurts so much as I have highlighted above. Please know that it is essential to honour your own story and proceed with patience and care as you follow the paw prints on your heart. The love all the way on the other side is waiting for you.

Honour your story.

Grief hurts. It takes time to heal. It changes you. It demands that you acknowledge your feelings and emotions. It takes all your energy and joie de vivre. But if you pause and remember that without the grief there is no love, you may feel the love that remains in your heart more. Your furry friend now asks that you redirect the unconditional love that they hold for you to heal yourself.

 PINK PET REFLECTIONS: YOUR PATH OF GRIEF

Stop, take a deep breath and reflect. Give yourself permission to go inward, access your Inner Pink Star and the paw prints on your heart. Follow their lead all the way home to the pure, unconditional love of two souls connected as one, holding a love that never dies as you heal your loss, feel the love and appreciate the lessons, knowing that *the whole point is love!*

The Path of Grief

Honour yourself and your pet by acknowledging and recording your feelings in your Pink Pet Grief Journal as you ponder the questions below. They are designed to help you understand why pet grief is so raw and difficult and to become aware of how each relates to your situation, feelings and heart.

Write what comes to your heart when you read the following:

- How does my grief feel? What feelings am I experiencing? Am I able to express my emotions?
- Do I feel a void? Can I simply just be with this void as the grief moves through me?
- Can I permit my grief to have a voice?
- What is the grief asking of me? What is most difficult for me at this point?
- Can I let grief do its thing? If so, what does it need right now?
- What do I miss the most about my pet?
- Has societal conditioning added to my grief?
- Are people making inappropriate comments to me about my loss? Can I distance myself from these comments and seek support from people who understand pet grief? If so, who are they?
- Was my pet linked to any major life events? What role did they play in my life? How does this add to my grief?
- Am I ready and willing to follow the paw prints through the grief to the love and lessons that await me?

- Am I able to provide the self-care and love needed to take the grief journey?
- Am I able to simply honour my loss and grief despite all the difficulties?

Give yourself a chance to assimilate and understand your responses. Sit with them for some time perhaps before you continue. Remember, this is a very difficult time and it is normal to feel deep levels of grief.

Once you are ready, let's move to *Part 2 The Love*, so you can learn more about the human-animal bond and the enduring unconditional love your pets leave in the form of paw prints scattered all over your heart.

LOSS CONTEMPLATIONS

- However your grief presents itself – a long, winding, misunderstood and tumultuous road or a sudden catapult into the grief where you struggle to find your ground – know that your story is a beautiful and heartfelt love story of two souls connected as one, holding a love that never dies.

- If you are still standing in the aftermath of your loss, feeling heartbroken, empty, sorrowful and alone, know that this is a normal phase of grief. Pet loss cuts deep yet walking through the grief journey, following the paw prints on your heart, is necessary to move forward.

The Path of Grief

- 🐾 Societal conditioning can make raw grief so much more difficult, as can the links to life events our pets join us with. Permitting your grief to have a voice and listening to it, including feeling the associated emotions, is imperative for you to proceed through the grief in a healthy way to find the love.

- 🐾 You may handle your loss differently to mine, but I hope both Max's and my story mirrored your grief somewhat and you can now trust that others do understand. You have the right to feel your grief, and in doing so you are honouring your pet and can begin to heal your loss.

- 🐾 At the end of the journey through all your grief and loss is love. In the next part, *The Love*, we will look a little more at that love and how, without grief, there is no love; they work so painfully yet beautifully together.

Heal the loss!

Pink Pet Love Note

You were three weeks shy of fifteen years old on your passing. I always wanted to make cupcakes for your special birthday. I hope instead you enjoyed your chocolate chip biscuit and ice cream party, a snippet of lightness before we said our goodbyes...

PART 2

The Love

The Love-Grief Dichotomy

"Until one has loved an animal a part of one's soul remains unawakened."

—Anatole France

The human-animal bond is filled with love!

It is a mutually beneficial and dynamic relationship between a human and an animal. It positively influences the physical, emotional, mental and spiritual wellbeing of both.

This relationship has existed for thousands of years, yet has become stronger and more validated in recent years. This bond has been researched, proven and recognised by many research papers, citations and studies. Ask an animal lover about the human-animal bond and they will passionately explain it away for hours... better than any doctorate paper. Why? Because *the whole point is love!*

When you lose your pet, you may fear that that love is gone forever, that the human-animal bond you had is gone. But here is the secret for grief survival: as you travel through your grief, you will access that love again. You see, love and grief are two sides of the same coin, and the human-animal bond, I believe, is forever.

Human-Animal Bond

"A dog is the only thing on earth that loves you more than he loves himself"

—Josh Billings

Every day, companion animals become more valued in our society and fill many roles in our lives. Many pet owners like myself consider our pet a fur child and a strong family member. We develop an unbreakable, deep bond with our furry family members and feathery friends. When your pet passes, how you react will have a lot to do with your relationship with them, how you valued them and what role they played in your life. Were they your best friend, child, childhood sweetheart, workmate, therapist, jogging/walking partner, support/therapy dog, movie-watching couch potato friend, travel companion, cuddle buddy, confidant, beach buddy or true love? Or all the above?

Did they listen to your deepest and darkest secrets and fears without judgement or reproach, giving instead many licks and hugs as support? Were they your social connection to the people in the park, the butcher where they sat for bits of fritz or your conversation point with passers-by who commented on their cuteness? This social connection, companionship and having someone to care for is imperative for the wellbeing of us as humans. When you lose this your life can fall into disarray. You not only lose your fur child but also your connection and possibly your reason for getting up in the morning. This can become more worrisome with the elderly when their pets are their whole life.

The Many Roles Our Pets Play

For some pet owners, their dogs are essential assistance dogs such as guide dogs, therapy dogs, hearing dogs, seizure dogs,

The Love-Grief Dichotomy

mobility assistance dogs, emotional support dogs and autism support dogs. Then there are the working dogs: police dogs, detection dogs, guard dogs, sniffer dogs, and search and rescue dogs. Military dogs are often decorated war heroes and get full military funerals, with their handlers often going to extreme efforts to bring their dog home to their country after their service.

Other examples we see are herding dogs, sled dogs or farm dogs that get extensive training to work the sheep or cattle. There is a never-ending list of roles our dogs and other pets play in our community, in our homes and in our hearts. The strong bonds that are built are heart-warming and heartbreaking when seemingly broken.

Working in the vet clinic, I would often hear amazing stories about the bonds between owners and their pets. The owners could not wait to share their pets' entertaining and sometimes lifesaving antics. Mostly, though, you could just see the gleam in each owner's eyes and their concern for their pet's health. I remember well on one occasion the owners of a German Shepherd explaining how the dog alerted the wife to the husband's approaching heart attack. According to the paramedics the dog saved his life. This was only one of many stories of love that were shared over my time at the clinic.

I have seen the local association working and training the autism dogs, and the way the dogs can settle and quieten a child in distress is extraordinary. What a lifesaving addition to the house for the child with autism, and for the parents and siblings to help them cope daily.

The human-animal bond is remarkable and never to be underestimated. Maybe, like me, you don't have any human children, so your fur children are proudly your 'child' and are treated and loved accordingly. They may go everywhere with you. You come home early because they are there, and you basically live to make their lives full and blessed. In caring for our pets we may project human thoughts, feelings and emotions onto them.

So, when they pass there is an empty vacuum. For me, it was as if one of my two children had died.

As pets weave themselves into our lives, we cohabitate with ease. We create a routine that works for both of us, catering for their needs and blending in ours. We teach them that we will return home each day and that the treat jar will never be empty, leaving them feeling safe in the knowledge that we will honour our promise to provide for them. This structure gives them and us safety and love as we live our life together.

We pet owners are often happier and healthier with a fur child despite everything being covered in fur. Studies confirm that to touch, hold, pat, cuddle or play with a pet reduces stress levels, lowers blood pressure, eases pain, improves mood and reduces loneliness. I believe this isn't all just a coincidence. The gifts our pets bring into our lives are intrinsic to their purpose in life.

A PURPOSEFUL LOVE

Your beloved pets have one purpose in their short but beautiful lives: to provide and teach you about all the ins and outs of unconditional love. In doing so, they lift your spirits and bring joy to your life. They do it so perfectly, with grace and dignity. Regardless of what you do, how long you leave them at home, how many treats you hand out in a day and if you let them sleep on the bed or not, unconditional love will always be directed your way. They cherish you as you cherish them. Each comes with their dharma and each fulfils it. It is up to you if you are open to receive the lessons that they gift you, in their living and in their passing.

LOVE!

This is the human-animal bond, and the *whole point is love!*

Your furry loved one's little heart beats only to please you. Those puppy dog eyes are all about making sure they bring joy to your life. Sometimes they

The Love-Grief Dichotomy

dig up the garden, chew your shoes, bark incessantly or wee inside. But all those things are just what dogs do; they know no different. We call it naughty, but they don't understand. They are a dog.

Until we take the time and effort, and show patience, compassion and understanding, to teach them how to be a good dog, they will know no better. They don't know our human rules unless we show them what to do. The more we can understand this, the more patience we can have with them. When they do wrong it's more about us not teaching them the right way. All they want to do is please us. So the more we can gently reinforce and reward their positive behaviour and ignore their negative behaviour, over and over, the better-behaved pet we will have.

Your pets wait for you while you are at work all day, and the minute you open the door their excitement cannot be contained. Their person is home and they can't get enough. No one is ever as excited to see you every day, no matter what has happened during their day. They just love you to bits. No games, just a massive showing of love every day.

They are willing to forgive, to support, to sit with you as you ponder life. They never judge you and accept everything sent their way. They respect and obey you (presuming you have trained them well) and continue to always be loving. Most humans cannot replicate the type of unconditional love we receive from our furry friends. Their innocence, vulnerability and desire to please, alongside their unconditional love, is a big reason why losing them is so excruciatingly painful.

Understand that the love sits deeply in your heart, and you can tap into it always. It's beautiful and pure and, consequently, it's the depth of that love that causes your grief to be equally deep. Love and grief are two sides of the same coin – a dichotomy that you will face each time you experience the passing of someone you love. It's then your responsibility to process this grief while holding onto the love. You can do it. I did, with both my father and Max. Let me share some more of my love-grief story with Max.

Pink Pet Love Note

Enjoy the drops, wriggles and rolls at Rainbow Bridge. Rustle up a storm with your renewed health, mobility and vigour. Please don't wait for me at the gate. Play with your friends and I will find you when I arrive. Until then I have the beautiful legacy you gifted me – unconditional love – and for that I'm everlastingly grateful...

Max's Empty Collar

When I arrived home from the vet clinic, everything felt strange and uneasy, like a weird and surreal dream. My world had been turned upside down. I kept expecting to see Max hot on my heels each time I moved, but sadly not. Suzy trailed around behind me with her tail down. She was missing Max as much as I was and hated being apart from him. They had always been together except for the last few weeks while I was away.

I placed his empty lead and collar onto the kitchen table like a sacred offering, positioning it onto what began my shrine to Lord Max. I treated his collar as fragile and delicate as it embodied everything about Max, the love I held and how I felt inside. His collar was one of the few physical tokens I now had to hold that linked me to him. It felt like a holy relic.

The Love-Grief Dichotomy

I didn't know what to do with myself. The emotions that arose were so strong; they left me shaking and highly anxious. Yet my body and my movements were slow, like a movie on half speed as I drifted aimlessly around the house. Everywhere I looked was covered in Max's fur, an emotional reminder of his absence.

It was beyond surreal. I felt totally disconnected from my body. I think I was in shock, and jet lag added to my despondency. I was sitting with him only hours earlier while he pawed me and breathed softly in his sleep – and now he was gone! How was that possible? My heart could not catch up with my new reality. I went to bed, but sleep eluded me as I sobbed non-stop with Suzy sleeping by my side. The pain was overwhelming.

My journal was the only thing that provided temporary relief from my emotions. I selected a beautiful journal with a cover depicting a field with green grass and clear blue skies. Perfect for Max! He loved his daily drops, wriggles and rolls at the park. One day, he had rolled so feverishly on the freshly cut wet grass that his golden fur turned a light tinge of green. He surfaced as the Incredible Hulk doggy style.

In the coming weeks and months, I wrote and wrote for what seemed like hours about the events of the last month, my feelings and my love for him. I bargained, I raged, I cried, I grieved. I hoped that the more I wrote and cried the more my grief would clear. But it just kept coming, bowling me over, with no reprieve yet.

Meanwhile, I felt Max in whatever room I entered, plunging instantly into the grief. At this stage, Max was on my mind every minute, and this lasted for a long time. The tears of grief were always flowing unless I was out and about and they became wedged in my throat. Then, when I was alone again, the valve at my throat would release and allow the tearful flow to continue.

The heaviness and intensity of this level of grief was new to me... and frightening. But from my professional studies, I understood that this was all normal and I had to follow the path of grief, surrender to it and let it do its thing. I had to let the grief energy move through my body and eliminate it, bit by bit. It would ultimately take me to the place I yearned to be. The place where I could capture and connect to the love in my heart, with smiles, laughter and love for our memories instead of being forever shrouded in sobs and suffering.

I chose not to repress or suppress any emotion that arrived. I did not want to remain numb to my feelings, our love or my life, and I knew this was likely to happen if I did.

Let grief do its thing.

I love my home, but for a time it only brought darkness and misery. I cringed each time I arrived home without Max at the gate or door with his beaming enthusiasm and big clown smile to greet me. I missed calling his name and watching him trotting devotedly towards me with his toenails clipping the floorboards and his ears flapping. I felt so alone despite Suzy constantly by my side. It felt like something was always missing and of course there was. It didn't feel like home without Max. Max made my house a home.

We had been through many challenging times together and he was my support system. He always made me smile.

The Love-Grief Dichotomy

When he was a young puppy, I nearly lost him to my ex-partner when we separated. Luckily, the angels were on my side and spoke to my inner wisdom, guiding me to take him to live with me despite my fragility at the time. He was my baby boy, my man, my fur child. It was his life purpose to be my boy and be bonded inextricably to me. Now he was gone.

It was time to decide on a home burial or a cremation. I decided on cremation with an urn, finally picking one from the many on offer – a pewter charcoal urn with silver paw prints, symbolising the paw prints he left on my heart. I loved it.

I chose to close the urn. I didn't want to scatter the ashes as I wanted him with me always, and I believed he would want the same. I was to collect the urn and Max in about five days, the longest five days of my life.

So, now he moves around the house, sitting in different sunny spots depending on my mood. Around it hangs a silver chain with a tag and his name proudly embossed on it in big letters: MAX!

The vet clinic was amazing. Even though I worked there I was treated like a normal client, and all the clients receive special treatment when they lose a fur child. You see, the staff in the vet clinics I was privileged to be in are all very devoted and highly intuitive to the pets and the grieving pet parents' needs. They rally around and are experts at providing care, knowing exactly the right supportive things to say.

I received a beautiful sympathy card signed by all the staff and they made a donation on Max's behalf to a relevant research organisation. Luckily, I worked in the vet industry where it is accepted that a pet is a family member and that losing them can be as traumatic as any other loss. I was able to take a couple of days off work for bereavement leave (though I don't think it is generally enough).

My bereavement leave, as short as it was, helped prepare me for the upcoming long, winding grieving process that followed.

Pink Pet Love Note

I think about our beautiful memories and ache to live them all over again, changing nothing. I feel blessed to have had you in my life and miss terribly the wet mohawk hairdos you wore so distinguishably...

Loving Grief Models

"When we think of those companions who travelled by our side down life's road, let us not say with sadness that they left us behind, but rather say with gentle gratitude that they once were with us."

—Unknown

Grief is a process. Like any process, there is a series of actions or steps that need to be taken to arrive at the particular outcome you are seeking. But grief differs in that you may oscillate back and forth between the different stages, miss some entirely, fly through others, repeat some or even get stuck in specific stages as you follow the path. The important thing with grief is to follow its lead.

Let grief do its thing. Surrender to the journey, listen to your inner guide and be very gentle with yourself. Honour this time in your life by creating space for your expression of grief and allow yourself to feel all the icky and tricky emotions that occur along the way. This is where taking bereavement leave can be very beneficial. What a perfect time to read through this book and to be guided on what's ahead!

Feeling emotions that rise without applying analytical attachment and judgement is a vital part of the journey. Yes, it hurts; it is agonising. But the emotions surface to be healed so you can ultimately access the love that underlies them at the end of your grief journey. Without grief there is no love. So, it makes sense that by allowing the turbulence and feeling the hurt you will eventually process the grief, returning to the love underneath.

It takes time and energy to move through this process. There is an old myth that says 'You will be okay. It just takes time'. It is not time alone, however. You also need to invest your energy in healing. It is unlikely you will heal fully without facing the grief with a strong commitment to work through it.

To understand a little more about your journey through grief is to understand a little more about grief itself, making the ride gentler or at least a little easier to navigate. There is no map. There is only a series of possible steps (aspects of grief) to become familiar with so that when different feelings and situations arise, you can acknowledge what grief wants from you. You can then act accordingly.

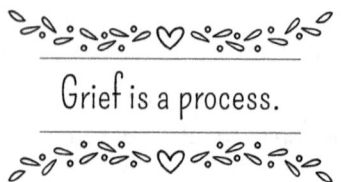
Grief is a process.

To feel it is to process it. To process it is to express it. To express it is to start to heal it.

As you progress through the process remember that each individual grieves differently. The same individual may also grieve differently in different situations. Remember this and allow yourself self-love and self-care. Self-love is the ability to be gentle and compassionate with yourself despite your grief. You make decisions that are right for you with trust and faith while accepting, loving and honouring the person who you are. You are the best person to deal with your grief. Even though you may reach out to others for help, ultimately only you know what your heart, soul and grief are calling out for.

Trust in your own journey through the pain. Don't allow others to cause you to stray off your path. Follow your own set of paw prints to the love awaiting you. This is where the torment of loss subsides. The sadness stays, but the grief journey propels you towards a rich and fulfilling life, allowing healing and transformation through your grief journey.

This section introduces you to two grief models that provide invaluable, supportive information on moving through the grief. These two models can be used in conjunction very well to create an overall understanding of grief and a way to process it. The first, a five-stage model of grief, was created by Swiss-born psychiatrist Elisabeth Kübler-Ross and first discussed in her book *On Death and Dying* (1969). It provides a good road map of the grief journey. The second, In the Pink Process (ITP Process), was designed by me and shared in my other books, *Heartbreak, Healing and Happiness* and *Grief, Grace and Gratitude*. I have applied it numerous times in my own life and with clients. These two fundamental models provide the tools to teach you all you need to know in theory to heal your grief.

Read, learn and digest all this information and then put it into practice to begin your own personal healing journey. It won't necessarily lessen the emotional quotient, but the information will definitely help you navigate your grief journey with more ease. You will feel more in control. There will still be steep cliffs, deep valleys and many potholes, but the tips and tools in these models will arm you with information to prepare for, and deal with, these climbs and falls when they appear.

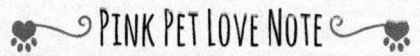

Pink Pet Love Note

Forever separate in body but forever linked through our heart and soul. We are never apart. I follow each paw print on my heart as you guide me through our memories about all the things you always knew, and I am only just learning...

FIVE STAGES OF GRIEF

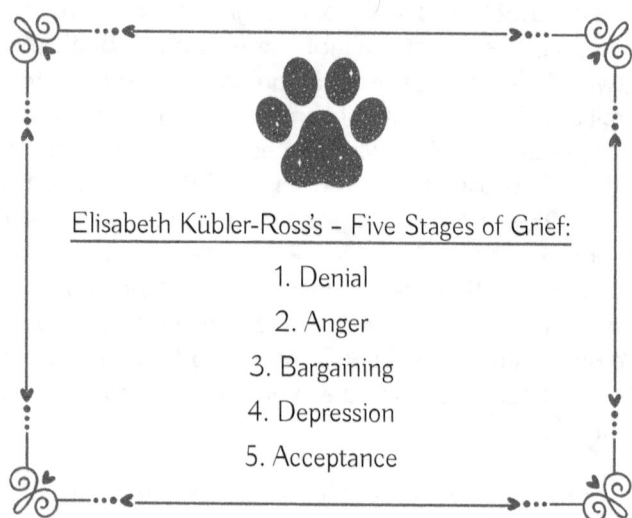

Elisabeth Kübler-Ross's – Five Stages of Grief:

1. Denial
2. Anger
3. Bargaining
4. Depression
5. Acceptance

Grief is a journey and, while each person's experience of grief will differ, it does help to understand the general stages of grief you may go through and how to navigate them. Initially created for terminally ill patients, Elisabeth Kübler-Ross's five-stage model explains the emotions before and near to death. She later expanded her model to include any form of loss such as the loss of a loved one. Hence I feel an explanation of these stages will be of great value to you on your grief journey.

The model describes what is to be expected in response to a loss. You may flow between one stage and another. You may not go through all the stages or you may go through some or all stages many times. You could remain at each stage for different time frames, and some may be more intense and seemingly destructive than others. They all have one shared element, however; each stage allows you to process your grief and move the grief energy through your body, heart and soul.

Loving Grief Models

Your experience will be different to others'; we all grieve individually. Grieving a pet can be different or the same as grieving a human. Again, it is a personal experience. Be mindful of this and gentle with yourself as you journey through the five stages of grief.

Stage 1. Denial

This is not happening to me...

Denial is the first stage of grief, where you experience shock, disbelief and confusion. This stage helps you survive your massive loss. It is a stage where you may refuse to accept your reality and your loss, with a voice inside reciting repetitively, "This is not happening to me". You do this to protect yourself from the initial shock and the overwhelming emotions about to arise.

You may feel numb and dazed, and wonder how you will cope. This stage allows you to slowly assimilate the loss and move through the initial stages of grief. You will begin to move out of denial and into the onslaught of emotions. This is a normal part of the grief journey.

Stage 2. Anger

Why me? Aarrgghh...

As the denial wears off, your ghastly reality will set in. Deep inside, you are more vulnerable than ever and hurting so much you may redirect this internal pain and find someone to blame for your pain and loss. You may feel angry at yourself, others, the vet or the world in general.

Rationally, you may understand that blame is illogical; however, your emotions will override your rational thinking. Your anger needs to be felt to move forward. It is the emotion that covers most of your other emotions and underlying hurt, which in time will surface to be dealt with. The anger often brings you out of your numb denial into a rainbow of emotions. The more you allow yourself to feel the anger the sooner it will begin to dissipate. This is a normal part of the grief journey.

Stage 3. Bargaining

If only...

Your loss makes you feel like you have lost control of your control. You feel vulnerable and powerless and are looking to gain some type of inner control of your world. Endless 'What if...' or 'If only...' statements dominate your thoughts. More than ever, you want life to return to what it was with your furry loved one by your side. You may consider what you would do if you had another chance. You can begin to feel guilty for your decision, for things you didn't do or see sooner, and initiate more internal pain through self-loathing. You may even bargain with a higher power to change your reality. It may not seem rational, but that is the randomness of grief. This is a normal part of the grief journey.

Stage 4. Depression

What's the point?...

During this stage, you may feel disconnected, sad, afraid, regretful and numb. Common symptoms of depression set in as you feel overwhelmed and weighed down with the loss. You may withdraw and avoid communication with others. As a result, grief enters your life at a deep level. This stage can be where you look to facilitate some sort of internal goodbye. Depression from a loss is an appropriate response at this stage of the grief journey and healing process. This is a normal part of the grief journey.

> Each stage is a normal part of the grief journey.

Stage 5. Acceptance

I think I can cope...

At this stage, you feel pulled to re-engage in life and social activities. You begin to move forward, slowly and delicately. It does not necessarily mean you are happy, but you have surfaced from your depression and feel a little lighter. You have accepted that the loss is now part of your new reality. You do not like it but can live with it.

Some people may never reach this stage. They stay locked in anger, sadness and blame. Not feeling and moving through your grief can keep you stuck in earlier stages and never allow you to find the peace and calm of acceptance. This peace is available to everyone upon moving gently through the stages of grief. This is a normal part of the grief journey.

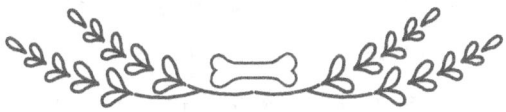

The stages of grief are not pleasant and can be difficult and complex. The grief is resting inside, just below the surface, and until you allow it to surface you cannot start to create healing. Avoidance only worsens the grief. Conversely, honouring yourself by understanding and starting to walk through this delicate part of your life will ultimately bring the peace and calm that is presently elusive.

Become familiar with the stages listed above to recognise where you are residing on any day. Be aware that your emotional climate and moods can change instantly, swaying from anger and sadness to snippets of peace and then back again. Grief may come to the surface gently or in crashing waves. Being aware may make it a little easier and prevent you from feeling like you are going crazy. Let me reassure you that you are not; you are grieving a deep loss.

Pink Pet Reflections: Stages of Grief

Stop, take a deep breath and reflect. Give yourself permission to go inward, access your Inner Pink Star and the paw prints on your heart. Follow their lead all the way home to the pure, unconditional love of two souls connected as one, holding a love that never dies as you heal your loss, feel the love and appreciate the lessons, knowing that *the whole point is love!*

Honour yourself and your pet by acknowledging and recording your feelings in your Pink Pet Grief Journal as you ponder the questions below.

- Which stage of grief am I currently in?
- Which stages if any have I already experienced?
- Can I recognise the different stages?
- Is there a particular stage that appears elusive to me?

In the Pink Process

In the Pink Process (ITP Process):

Step 1: Awareness

Step 2: Responsibility

Step 3: Feeling

Step 4: Forgiveness

Step 5: Acceptance

The information on the ITP Process that I present here is similar to that in my other books. If this is the first time you have read it then digest it and use it to help your grief. If it is the second or third time you have read about this process, the information will continue to help you learn about loss, grief and your inner self.

By now you know that the journey to heal your pet loss can be as intense and painful as any other type of loss. So you need to process the grief equally to other major grief events in your life. The love of you and your pet deserves that. You can use the ITP Process tools during your pet grief and in times of other heartbreak and loss to help you develop emotionally and heighten your emotional intelligence. The tools will provide a foundation and structure to rebuild yourself through your grief journey and will stay with you forever like the memories of your fur child.

I used this process three times in three years: during a devastating relationship breakup; on this occasion when I lost my Max; and again when I lost my dad. Each situation presented differently in my life and each was a different type of grief. However, the process for me was the same. It didn't necessarily lessen the emotional response, but it provided a structure and understanding of what I was going to go through. It provided me with a few tools to prop myself up and move me through the treacle-like grief that threatened to keep me stuck at many points, one tiny paw print at a time.

These valuable tools will open your heart and eyes to a structure or path, providing you with a few tools to prop you up while you feel yourself hanging on the edge of the grief cliff. You may not necessarily go through the five steps in the order I present them. The grief response to the loss of your fur child is your individual story so just allow it to unfold the way it presents itself. Use this process as a guide and another learning experience only, to become more connected to yourself, remain connected to your loved one and begin the healing grief journey. Opening yourself to an understanding of grief will open your heart to heal. Opening your heart to heal ultimately opens your heart to love again.

Let me now guide you through the five steps of the ITP Process in more depth, including my own experience with it, while I stay beside you at every step. My hope is that the ITP Process will give you a place to begin, as it did me.

Pink Pet Love Note

Max, I miss saying, "Max, bedtime! Let's take your booties off". Goodnight Max, I love you. I feel blessed to have had you in my life for nearly fifteen years. You taught me unconditional love. You were always there. I am forever grateful...

Loving Grief Models

In The Pink Process Step 1: Awareness

To honour myself, my grief and my emotions, I found that I first needed to create *awareness* for where I was and what I was feeling. So out came my pen and journal and I began to write profusely, seeking what lay within through awareness. This awakening process allowed me to reveal my thoughts, feelings and truths to myself. This was the first step in the ITP Process and indeed the first step to profound internal change.

Awareness is the key to being truthful with yourself. Awareness opens your eyes, ears, heart and mind to what is happening within, be it good or not so good. This awareness of your inner landscape allows your experience to shine through. You begin to see your truth and understand it is beneficial for the suffering to surface rather than bury it in avoidance or ignorance.

If you are at the start of your grief, you most likely do not know exactly what you are feeling. You may be experiencing new and unwanted thoughts and emotions and feeling like you are being held prisoner by them. This is normal. Developing awareness and being mindful of your thoughts, emotions, feelings, behaviours, choices and all other areas of your life will assist you to make more informed decisions about your grieving and your environment. You can then start to be more authentic, take back some power and gain some control.

There are three main areas to be aware of:

- *Be aware of what you are thinking.*

    Thoughts dictate how you feel, and feelings dictate how you behave. Notice when thoughts pop into your head and write down any concerning thoughts you may want to revisit later. Just let the thoughts swirl around in your head but be mindful of them. Try not to attach to them and be taken on a downward spiral. Become the observer. Take notice. Be aware.

- 🐾 *Be aware of what you are feeling.*

    Sit with your feelings and acknowledge them. In doing so, allow them to flow through you naturally. (In ITP Step 3 you will learn more about expressing those feelings.) Journal about your feelings to help ease confusion. Become the observer. Take notice. Be aware.

- 🐾 *Be aware of your behaviours.*

    Notice what you are doing, what you are not doing, what you are saying, how you are treating others and how you are treating yourself. Again, be the observer. Take notice. Be aware.

Awareness brings honesty, authenticity and truth. This can result in tough decisions being made that have consequences. Being aware of your grief and being truthful with yourself is a big responsibility. Yet when you follow its lead through your grief, you can live an authentic grief journey and ultimately an authentic life.

> Awareness brings honesty, authenticity and truth.

To have awareness through your grief journey takes courage. Grief taps into your vulnerabilities and can add to feelings of powerlessness. Know that the strength you had before the loss is still available to you. It is just lying dormant, overshadowed by the intense grief emotions.

Don't get me wrong. This stage can be challenging. I initially found awareness difficult. I lived with both awareness and denial. I was also in shock, struggling to comprehend my reality of loss. I kept expecting to see Max at the gate, on his bed or wandering around the house and hovering at the food cupboard. When I fed Suzy each night, Max's empty food bowl grazed my already aching heart. Our normal daily routines had been severed and left instead

Loving Grief Models

bizarre feelings, kind of like walking around in a grey misty fog, struggling to find something to hold onto.

I framed one of his paw print cards and a swatch of his fur and sat with it for hours at the kitchen table. I remembered and felt. It sat next to his empty collar, adding to Lord Max's shrine. I continued to add beautiful photos, two photo albums and a framed photo of Max in the park, his favourite place. His shrine was like an altar that was growing with all his memorabilia. I looked at the photos of his last day over and over. Waves of deep grief kept bowling me over. It was surreal, completely disorientating and confusing – yet very, very real. Heart-shatteringly real.

Awareness can help you acknowledge the enormity of your situation and the depth of your hurt. Without this awareness, things may continue to feel surreal whereby you disconnect from yourself and deny your feelings and emotions, locked in your grief cycle that in time can lead to more complicated grief.

To heal and continue your journey through life, it is necessary to go through the season of grief. To do this you need to develop awareness, not just in grief but in life. You can go on to honour those you have lost and those you lose in the future, be it your fur friends or human family members or friends. It is a deep mark of respect for your pet and yourself to grant yourself entry into the gruelling grief journey, which starts with awareness.

Give yourself permission to start here. One day and one piece of awareness at a time.

Be proud of yourself for taking the lonely pet grief journey despite others undervaluing or minimising it. You are on a tough road, and just by being on it you are courageous and self-honouring. Admitting that you feel proud of yourself may make you teary. Many things can make you feel teary including thoughts about your pets, places, people, situations, memories, movies, music and just the grief. Remember, you are now most likely overly sensitive and vulnerable, so it doesn't take much to start the tears rolling.

Even a micro-moment of pride, which is self-love in disguise, can create a stream of tears. Allow them to flow; this is a healthy, normal part of grief.

For me, everything good and not so good made me cry for an awfully long time. The bond between every dog and owner I saw made me sad as it represented what I had lost. But it also filled me with warm, fuzzy feelings because I was truly coming to understand, and fully felt, the unconditional love Max had gifted me.

Eventually, those tears of grief became tears of beauty. Sometimes I swung between both. Allow the free flow of sadness and love to spill from your heart, water your soul and start to wash the grief away.

 ## Pink Pet Reflections: Building Awareness

Stop, take a deep breath and reflect. Give yourself permission to go inward, access your Inner Pink Star and the paw prints on your heart. Follow their lead all the way home to the pure, unconditional love of two souls connected as one, holding a love that never dies as you heal your loss, feel the love and appreciate the lessons, knowing that *the whole point is love!*

Honour yourself and your pet by acknowledging and recording your feelings in your Pink Pet Grief Journal as you ponder the questions below around awareness.

- 🐾 Am I aware of my thoughts, feelings and actions?
- 🐾 If not, am I willing to create awareness of my thoughts, feelings and actions?

- 🐾 Do I give myself permission to access my awareness of my grief journey?
- 🐾 What can I do to increase my awareness of my grief?
- 🐾 Can I to listen to what my grief is telling me and asking of me?

Review the words and feelings you have expressed and take some time out for yourself.

In The Pink Process Step 2: Responsibility

The revelations I uncovered through my growing awareness and reflection gave me an opportunity to own my thoughts, feelings, choices, grief and behaviours. It moved me on from victimhood and a blaming mentality. I took a small amount of control back and realised I had started the healing journey. Next, I had to take *responsibility* to take this journey – the second ITP step. I didn't want to travel it but knew that, despite everything, it was best for me to do so.

Once you take this step, you are becoming the author of your life. Taking responsibility is tough! Some days it just seems more fitting to stay wrapped in ignorance, surrounded by denial and in a bubble of unawareness. However, this means you do not take responsibility for your healing and instead hinder it.

You are most likely not responsible for the loss of your furry loved one. Even if you opted for euthanasia and feel the guilt, remember that it was an act of love to save your pet from their pain and to allow them dignity in their passing. I believe making this decision to remove your pet's pain while plunging into your own is the biggest expression of love.

You are, however, responsible for what happens now, that is, how you respond or react to your loss and how you continue to live your life. It is your decision now to either take responsibility or not to that will determine whether your heart opens or remains closed to your future, shaping the rest of your life.

The life purpose of your heart is to give and receive love – with yourself, all sentient beings (human, furry, feathery, scaly, etc.) and our universe. Right now, your heart is shrouded in grief and may feel permanently closed – a normal response to loss. Be reassured that if you keep moving forward the love for your furry loved one buried below will slowly surface again when the time is right, filling your heart to the brim. This creates a softness and tenderness within you.

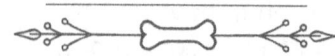

The life purpose of your heart is to give and receive pure love.

The grief process can allow your heart to feel more love than ever before, which is ultimately passed on to others and returned to yourself. To access and give away this love housed in your heart, your heart needs to be open and functioning well. To achieve this, you need to take responsibility. Although you can gain support from others to move towards healing, they cannot do it for you. You need to do that for yourself. This simply means saying to yourself, "I am responsible for my feelings, pain, suffering and healing". A simple statement but perhaps difficult to invoke if you are stuck in a cycle of victimhood.

ANGER, BLAME AND VICTIM MODE

You may be angry and blame others, avoiding the grief journey and looking within. Staying in blame mode can leave you feeling like a victim and removes self-responsibility in not allowing yourself to feel the hard feelings and walk towards healing. If you are in this victim mode, your feelings may depend on another person. When you place blame solely on another person, you may continue to use them to avoid feeling your feelings. They are an excuse. You instead continue to outwardly blame them for the incident and indirectly also for the way you are now feeling. Hence, you are

LOVING GRIEF MODELS

deflecting instead of taking responsibility for your own feelings, which ultimately are always your responsibility.

All of these dynamics can send you on a dangerous downward spiral to a more helpless state or even a deep depression. When you are not being authentic and not taking ownership of your feelings, you will sway back and forth in the grief breeze with even less control.

You might be right in blaming someone else. But to heal you need to look at your thoughts, feelings, emotions and behaviours (having awareness), and own them. Taking responsibility for your feelings removes you from victim mode and places you on the correct path to the next steps in the ITP Process and healing your grief.

You only get one life, and losing your fur child is tragic. They will never hover at your feet again. Their familiar traits and idiosyncrasies remain only in your memories and heart. Their lives are just too short, I know. Taking the grief journey may put your life on hold for a period, maybe a long time. It will possibly break you wide open and change you. But try and stay connected. Be aware. Be responsible.

TAKING OWNERSHIP

Taking responsibility will mean you are not only taking ownership of your grief but of your whole life. It determines how you walk to your future and how you allow your heart to give (and receive) love to other furry souls and people in the future.

At this stage, you may not know what beautiful lessons could arise from the loss of your pet. The secret is that wise choices will lead you to the healing peace you so desperately seek.

I walked towards taking responsibility for my grief and it continued me on my grief journey. A big part of this included returning to work after my bereavement leave. It was challenging. This was where I had last seen Max and left him safely with the staff. To know that his body was still on-site in a big cold freezer, waiting to be collected by the crematorium, was mind-boggling. I stood in the treatment room and noticed the harness they had used to lift him, which was still covered in his beautiful golden fur.

Being a staff member certainly had its benefits. However, during this stage of my grief it felt otherwise. I was surrounded by his passing everywhere. All our painstakingly perfected internal processes and procedures for pet cremations were being carried out under my nose. This time it was my pet, my Max, on all the reports and lists. I was experiencing what our clients go through firsthand; I was now on the other side of the process.

I was grateful that we were overscrupulous in dealing with pets' passing and cremations because I could now sit comfortably knowing the process would run smoothly. I knew from experience that Max's passing was viewed as sacred, as were all the emotions that come with it. The whole situation was dealt with delicate care by both the staff and me.

Learn to say, "I own this grief journey," even if you don't like it.

Learn to say, "I take responsibility for my grief," even if you don't like it.

Taking ownership and responsibility will strengthen you as you walk through the grief journey and keep you feeling connected to your true nature, to reflect love and gratitude. Give yourself permission to be the creator and author of yourself, your life and your grief journey. Take the path to healing that works best for you, allowing the love that is buried to slowly surface and shine.

As I returned to work, I didn't stop being aware of my feelings and continued being gentle with myself. I walked my path while inwardly dealing with the tremendous suffering of my loss. I encourage you to do the same. Continue to feel your grief while allowing self-love to flow. Allow your vulnerabilities and gentle side to lead you. This is the side of you that knows what it needs. It is the quiet voice inside directing you. To hear her, you need to remain still and quiet and be patient with yourself.

Pink Pet Reflections: Taking Responsibility

Stop, take a deep breath and reflect. Give yourself permission to go inward, access your Inner Pink Star and the paw prints on your heart. Follow their lead all the way home to the pure, unconditional love of two souls connected as one, holding a love that never dies as you heal your loss, feel the love and appreciate the lessons, knowing that *the whole point is love!*

Honour yourself and your pet and record your feelings in your Pink Pet Grief Journal as you ponder the questions below. They are a starting point for you to move towards taking ownership and responsibility.

- 🐾 Am I taking responsibility for my grief journey?
- 🐾 If not, am I deflecting responsibility through blaming others? What am I avoiding and what payoff am I receiving in my life right now by not taking responsibility?
- 🐾 What would I need to do differently if I took responsibility?
- 🐾 Am I now willing to begin taking responsibility for myself and my healing?
- 🐾 Can I say, "I own this grief journey. I take responsibility for my grief"?

Review the words and feelings you have expressed and take some time out for yourself.

In The Pink Process Step 3: Feeling

Having learnt to develop more awareness of your grief (Step 1) and to take responsibility for your grief journey (Step 2), you can now move on to the next step of the ITP Process: *feeling*. This is the key to shifting some of the intense grief energy. Feeling our feelings during grief sometimes verges on the threshold of impossible. But not quite!

When I moved onto the third ITP step and allowed myself to feel my feelings, the internal pressure was released and my healing continued. I began to understand and label my feelings and journal them. I learnt why they were there and what they were telling me. I had never experienced so many new and different emotions. I survived. Just!

You can believe me when I say that no matter what you are feeling and how far you have fallen, it is always possible to stand up, brush yourself off and climb back up that cliff face to continue the journey. I did it. It is possible to feel your feelings and not be forever ruined. In fact, it can be the opposite.

Each moment you repress your feelings you allow negative, anxious energy to be stored within you. Each bottled-up feeling creates more internal tension that you will eventually need to release. If you don't know how to do this in a healthy way, you may start developing negative behaviours and issues to absorb them.

Some feelings and emotions can be frightening and command your attention constantly. If you run and hide, they will chase you down and create all sorts of disharmony until you stop and listen. Once you acknowledge your feelings, as you learnt in Step 1, it helps you now to allow yourself to fully experience and release them. Your interlinked body, mind, emotions and soul will thank you enormously. This release creates more spaciousness and light and enables you to breathe freely once again, often removing the knot or pressure in your chest.

Loving Grief Models

Once you have experienced the intensity of these feelings and emotions a few times, it becomes easier to accept them. It is also easier if you know how to deal with them or, at least, just permit them to send their grieving energy through your body without resistance. You will feel lighter, more connected to yourself and more loving towards yourself. This is when the magical moments of peace, joy and happiness start to appear through the cracks of despair. You can then access some more free space to remember your pet fondly.

> The beauty lies beyond the difficult emotions.

Feeling your feelings may well be the one part of the entire process that is the most challenging. And rightly so. It is, however, the master key to moving forward. The beauty lies beyond the difficult and hurtful emotions. The unconditional love that has been gifted to you from your pet is there under all the pain. Working through the pain will offer a chance for the love to emerge, in time.

When I lost Max, I began to understand the depth and intensity of the grief journey. He was my first child. It was the first major loss I had experienced that produced so much grief. I had never cried so many tears. The enormity of the emotions continued to surprise me, but I eventually handed the reins over and surrendered to experiencing the feelings as part of my grief journey. This enabled the deep grief and emotional pain to begin to clear.

I had to learn how to allow the whole rainbow of emotions to run through my body such as anger, frustration, anxiety and sadness. I had to get comfortable with these tough emotions. It was not easy.

Find or Create a Nurturing Environment

As with any loss there come the attachments and links to the loss. I continued to take Suzy to the park. The first day back was the worst. I came face to face with all our park friends asking how my holiday was and where was Max. I hadn't prepared myself for the onslaught of questions, and verbalising the story was distressing. In hindsight, however, while traumatic this was another means to help express and process the grief. My park friends totally understood the depth of my loss as most of them had been there before. They all respected and adored Max and were more than happy for me to tell umpteen stories of his life and hilarious acts. It eventually became one of my most favourite spaces to go to because they got it, unlike so many others that didn't.

It's important, especially in the early days of the grief journey, to find environments that provide support and initiate healing for your fragile soul, instead of promoting further separation and aloneness. The park people were not necessarily my best friends or people I would normally have turned to for support, but at this time they were the right people to help me through because they understood. My 'Lord Max shrine' was also a special place where I could feel close to Max and thus closer to my feelings, allowing them to flow through me.

Pet siblings are feeling it too

We don't really know what sibling pets feel when they lose their friends. But we do know dogs are capable of love and are highly astute and intuitive. So I believe they feel the loss. They sense something has changed, and they miss their friend. They also may react to our feelings as they pick up on energy and sense our moods. For example, if I get cranky, Suzy's body cues instantly change as her anxiety levels rise. Her tail goes between her legs and she slinks away or starts to get agitated.

After Max's passing, I sensed Suzy was suffering her own pain too. She was a little lethargic. She seemed not to know what was expected of her, where Max was or why things were different. You see, dogs are creatures of habit and function as a good companion animal when they have a structure. So the first night I gave her Max's elevated food bowl – as she was getting older and it was time for her to upgrade – she was bamboozled. She stared at me then at the bowl full of food and then back to me again. She knew she was not meant to eat from Max's bowl. She had tried to polish his food off numerous times and I had always stopped her. This broke my heart all over again. I needed Max here to assure her that she was now allowed to use his bowl.

When I arrived home she would walk to the back of the car and just stand there looking at me, expecting him to jump out. With gentle encouragement, lots of hugs and pats and a lot of extra special time spent with her – she came most places with me for a time – she slowly came around.

When it comes to losing a pet sibling, some pets just get on with it like nothing has happened. For others it may not be so simple. Some may have a lack of appetite while others may display a lack of enthusiasm for their favourite things. Or maybe they temporarily forget their toilet training or become more anxious and clingier, struggling to adjust to their new environment. This could turn into separation anxiety where they begin to destroy things when left alone.

One of my mother's dogs hid under a chair in the bedroom for six months, only surfacing to eat or do his business. Each pet is different and highly intuitive, and we need to accommodate this. So please pay attention to your pet's body language and behaviour in certain situations, to gauge what emotions they are feeling and provide comfort. Be gentle and patient with them as they adjust. You may even need to remove them from situations as needed.

Animals are very intuitive.

To help Suzy to not be anxious or lonely during this transition, whenever I went out, I enriched her environment. I left the TV or radio on for company and I gave her things to keep her occupied. I had to be mindful of Suzy's grief and walk her through her own journey to ensure she healed healthily and didn't sprout new unwelcome and destructive behaviours.

I also had to be mindful of my displays of emotions without suppressing them. As our pets are so sensitive, I often took my overwhelming grief to another room so it would not be so upsetting and add to Suzy's stress.

The most important thing is to retain your pet's normal routine. Have a structure, continue to praise positive behaviours and ignore negative ones – the rule for positive reinforcement training. Be aware of what is happening for them; notice their behaviours. Care and nurture them but be careful not to overcompensate and provide too much extra attention else this can lead to separation anxiety or compounded anxiety. Especially if they are already prone to it.

Just like our grief, our pet's grief takes time. So give them that time to adjust to their new normal and speak with your vet if you become overly concerned. They are there to help you and your pet. Following are some of the many ways to help our pets.

ENVIRONMENT ENRICHMENT IDEAS

- daily walks, training sessions, park visits
- play dates with dogs and people
- rides in the car
- ball throwing and playtime
- bones, chew toys, Kong toys that can be filled with food or maybe peanut butter
- sandpit or paddling pool
- scattering their food outside and teaching them to find it (like a treasure hunt)
- fill toilet rolls with treats
- scrunch up some newspaper with treats

Loving Grief Models

- 🐾 dog ice blocks made with a stock cube, gravy or soup and frozen into a Kong toy or ice cube trays and left in the dog's bowl to defrost during the day.
- 🐾 newspaper knots – newspaper sheets rolled up and tied in a knot with treats inside.
- 🐾 other interesting, creative ideas that you come up with

Dealing with Anxiety and Anger

During your grief journey, you may find anxiety and anger arising. I certainly did! Anxiety surfaced amongst a plethora of fears:

- 🐾 I feared I wouldn't be able to cope with the grief and that I would forget Max – a fear that developed when I lost my dad also.
- 🐾 I feared life would never be the same and I would be unbalanced and grieving forever.
- 🐾 I was worried that others would think I was grieving too long for a dog. Even though I worked in the vet industry, society and its conditioning had even got to me.
- 🐾 I was worried I would never be able to face getting another furry friend.

I now know that anxiety is a normal human emotion, particularly during a stressful situation. It arises from thoughts creating havoc in your mind, throwing all kinds of 'What if...' questions your way that bring up deep worries. Anxiety symptoms can torment you, which is why most people try to run and hide from them. Anxious thoughts at their worst are usually ludicrous. They are like a big scary monster, but once you face them head on, they normally back down.

Anxiety demands authenticity when you are being inauthentic. Feeling highly stressed, people-pleasing and not listening to your needs will see anxiety heighten even further. The more you ignore and repress the anxiety, the more it will increase. In heightened anxiety, your body will scream at you to listen as it wants you to slow down and acknowledge your feelings. It will continue till you choose to hear its message.

When you choose to listen, anxiety can teach you many things. It has always been my guiding star, leading me inward and to look after myself. Until I had this epiphany I needed to deal with the anxiety and grief attacks as best I could, and there were many. Further on, I detail many different tools you can use to lessen and deal with your grief.

When anger and frustration surfaced, it was hard for me to understand and sit with these emotions, and even harder to just let them be. I felt angry, cranky or irritable a lot. While uncomfortable, this was a normal consequence of grief. I learnt to be in the moment of the feeling, whatever that happened to be. I learnt to accept and surrender to it. When I did, things inside gradually shifted and improved.

Burying your anger will keep toxic energy running through you and possibly complicate your grief. It will eat you up inside and make it impossible to access the love and other emotions housed within you. Accepting that anger is a part of the grief journey can allow your anger to move through you. Yell, vent and scream; do whatever you need to move the anger energy through you. When you do, it will start to fade and clear. You may notice things are a little better and that you feel a little lighter. This will enable you to access and harness the emotions that lie beneath the anger, like sadness.

Loving Grief Models

From sadness to love

The sadness I experienced beyond the anger and the anxiety was a gift. It enabled me to get in touch with my vulnerability and hurt. This emotion has always been easier for me to connect with. The hurt was so deep and heartbreaking, but I was finally ready to acknowledge this and cried endless streams of tears over what I had lost: Max!

I realised that my sadness represented all the love I felt I had lost, and for that I savoured it. It was all my love for Max rising to be felt and to keep me connected to him. I honoured each tear and its message and purpose. A softness and gentleness appeared within me, allowing me to feel closer to my soul, reconnecting to the love deep inside. I was waking up to the unconditional love Max had taught me. Our love, my love that had been shrouded by grief! It felt beautiful despite the tears. I finally understood what it represented and how it felt.

Like me, you may experience so many emotions waiting to surface to allow healing to start. They will come with pain, insights and finally, much later, love. That I can assure you! My emotional rainbow included more difficult feelings and emotions than I ever imagined before losing Max. Unleashing these, however, allowed a spectrum of new loving and spectacular emotions to rise in their intensity also.

By feeling the full range of your negative emotions, in this step, you get to experience the entire rainbow of emotions and tap into the beautiful, loving and miraculous emotions buried below. Feel the anxiety, anger, sadness and all the emotions in between and around, then the expansive loving emotions like joy, bliss, contentment, happiness and love follow soon afterwards. To process grief there is no way around this; it is the master key to your healing and happiness. If you can only learn one lesson let this be it.

Loss, Love and Lessons

Allowing yourself to feel your emotions is the biggest gift you can give yourself. It will bring healing, connection to your loved one, a deeper connection to yourself and your true essence and ultimately a richer life.

To integrate grief fully into your being, each feeling that arises needs to be given space and respect to move through you. To process your feelings, firstly stop. Remember the first ITP step to be aware of what is swilling around inside. Then the second ITP step to take responsibility. Next, feel the emotions as you immerse yourself in them. As they arise naturally by expressing them: cry, yell, scream, laugh. Repeat as needed. A little piece of healing will take place each time.

To help understand and see the benefit of feeling my feelings and emotions I use this little equation: STOP, Be aware, Feel, Express, Heal. Stopping gives us space to acknowledge what is happening, and then we need to use our awareness to go within and see what is swilling around. Next, we feel the emotions – cry, yell, shake – whatever we need to do while not hurting ourselves or others. The expression of them is then what moves us to a healing state.

Most importantly, remember to be gentle with yourself. One step at a time. Don't push yourself. You are in a learning phase, a time when we are sometimes clunky. Let yourself make mistakes. In time and with practice, living life in your new way will become easier and more natural. Very soon you will be ready for the next step: Forgiveness.

Pink Pet Reflections: My Feelings

Stop, take a deep breath and reflect. Give yourself permission to go inward, access your Inner Pink Star and the paw prints on your heart. Follow their lead all the way home to the pure, unconditional love of two souls connected as one, holding a love that never dies as you heal your loss, feel the love and appreciate the lessons, knowing that *the whole point is love!*

Honour yourself and your pet by pondering the questions below that will take you directly to your feelings. Record your feelings in your Pink Pet Grief Journal.

- 🐾 What emotions are most prominent for me right now?
- 🐾 Am I able to let my emotions flow through me?
- 🐾 Do I feel in shock, in denial, angry, sad, anxious, depressed? What other emotions am I feeling?
- 🐾 Do I feel alone? If so, how can I feel more connected?
- 🐾 Am I considering my remaining pet's feelings and anxieties?

Review the words and feelings you have expressed and take some time out for yourself.

In The Pink Process Step 4: Forgiveness

Finding *forgiveness* for yourself and others is the fourth ITP step after gaining an understanding of your feelings. Once I took that step, I began to forgive myself for any acts that were not in line with self-love. I was also able to inspect internally if I had laid any inappropriate blame. Finding forgiveness can be particularly difficult, especially through the pet loss journey as we may carry the burden of added guilt following euthanasia. Forgiveness is complex!

During your grief, as mentioned before, you may be angry and blame a myriad of people: the vet, family, friends, God, a stranger, yourself. Yet for true healing, it is necessary to understand how forgiveness is the kindest and most compassionate gift to yourself. Forgiveness puts your heart at peace and allows you to find small openings for the warmth and love to flow in. People may have done the wrong thing, acted against their values or your values, said the wrong thing, made a mistake and hurt you or your furry loved one. But that is now in the past.

Sometimes the blame may be attributed to the one you lost. How could they die and leave you behind and cause all the hurt? This style of thinking starts a rollercoaster of guilt or regret, bringing with it more complex emotions. Being angry with them can create anger towards yourself and guilt for being angry at them. It can be a vicious cycle. All the emotions start piling up like a giant Jenga tower waiting to topple over. You might even feel like you are going crazy. Your mind is not your own.

You may hold tremendous guilt in your heart over your decisions that led to their passing and now your pain, and you seem unable to shed this. Grief hijacks most of your common sense and, for a while, you are on grief autopilot. You may need to go inward and seek self-forgiveness.

Remember, if you made the choice to euthanise, you made the decision purely to release your furry loved one from their pain and suffering. You may question this decision now they have passed. This is when you can come back to the love. It was the vast love you had for them that enabled you to make this decision to kindly release them from their pain. It was a beautiful, loving act for your furry friend.

LOVING GRIEF MODELS

You may berate yourself because you felt you left the decision for too long, feeling they may have suffered unnecessarily. Many other thoughts may run through your mind as you process your loss that creates guilt. Something that works for me is to ask myself this question: "Did I do the best with what I knew and with the information I had at the time?" The answer is generally yes.

Try asking yourself that question too. You may be feeling guilt, but remember you would not have intentionally hurt your pet or caused them any discomfort. So remember you did the best with what you knew at the time, even if you know different now. When we are shrouded in stress, anticipatory grief and indecision, it is very hard to find the strength within to make the choices we need to make. We get confused and overwhelmed.

Be self-loving and gentle with yourself as you come to terms with this part of your grief. Gently forgive yourself and allow the guilt to fade away. Whoever you blame, keeping the anger and blame tucked inside will only cause more damage to your already fragile soul. Forgiveness changes this!

With Max, I knew in my heart the decision was the right one. The paw he had placed on the photo albums on our last day was his sign that it was time. It was not till later that day, when he had suffered more seizures, that my heart knew it was time. Knowing it was right beforehand still did not stop me from questioning my decision and holding guilt after the event.

Self-forgiveness is self-loving.

Around this time, I was sitting in our staff meeting and one of the exercises was based around the question, "If you could have one superpower what would it be?" My answer was to go back to a time when Max and I were together and sitting in the park on the green grass and I was watching him do his drops, wriggles and rolls. I just wanted to feel him by my side again. I was really struggling to let him go and I held an element of guilt too. Grief continues to appear and overcome you even from such simple questions or statements from others.

Once again, the vet reassured me that I had picked the right time and that Max had been suffering and was not going to improve. We had tried everything. Rationally, I knew this as vets take euthanasia seriously. They are advocates for preventative and curative treatment of animals while always considering the balance between extending an animal's life and prolonging its suffering. This did provide snippets of reassurance, but it still took me some time to release my guilt, create self-forgiveness and be gentle with myself.

It took time to realise that it was my immense love for him that helped make the decision. So how could it have been wrong? I found peace and forgiveness soon after.

Guilt over euthanasia

Pet owners find themselves facing a real predicament when it comes to euthanasia. When is the right time? I believe if you stop and listen to your heart, really feel it, the right time will be presented to you. You have such a close bond with your pet that you will just know. This has been the case for many people I have spoken to.

However, for many others it's different. Challenges like the following may get in the way:

- They just can't let go.
- They lack the confidence to make the decision.
- There are differing family opinions.
- They wonder if there is maybe another drug to try.
- They think others don't understand how much pain they are in.

Loving Grief Models

Or there could be numerous other reasons why they can't decide.

Our pets can't communicate how bad their pain is and they actually mask their pain well. This is something to consider in finding the right decision at the right time. The vets and nurses are the best ones to talk to about this and be guided by. But ultimately you need to be the one to decide. You are the pet parent, the mum or dad of your fur child. This is why it is so difficult and generally brings a heart filled with guilt, which is a very normal part of pet grief. So, it's important to spend some time feeling the emotions around this and releasing and forgiving yourself.

Forgiveness is not always about being right or apportioning blame. It is about living your life with a peaceful inner self free from burdens and suffering. Forgiveness provides this! It is a beautiful gift allowing you to acknowledge what has happened and to let it go. Forgiveness enables you to untie the bonds and attachments to a person, a decision, thoughts or a situation that keep you stuck in blaming mode.

In doing so, it will in turn remove the resentment, bitterness and toxic energy that it has been generating, allowing the inner wounds to heal. Following true forgiveness is lightness and inner spaciousness that feels pure, tender and loving.

It is a choice to forgive but not an easy one! Some people find it is easier to remain locked in limbo land where they have the convenience of focusing on something else other than themselves, thus avoiding responsibility. But residing in blame mode and refusing to contemplate forgiveness can be another guise for not moving forward. You willingly give control to others to manage your life and your feelings. You remain stuck in blame where you are angry and miserable rather than planning strategies or ideas to step you forward in your grief journey.

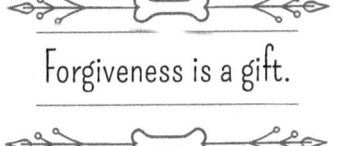

Forgiveness is a gift.

You may not know how to move forward, so staying there in blame mode may be what you are familiar with and thus it feels safer, even if it is uncomfortable. It may feel safer than stepping out into foreign territory, even if that dangles a chance of a better life and a better state of feeling. As humans, we like what we know regardless of its uneasiness.

However, an uncomfortable comfortableness can eat away at your spirit slowly and destroy your energy, passion and light, keeping your spirit fragmented. Inner love and peace remain elusive and you become miserable and negative. It may likely be the easiest way out but far from the loving and responsible way out. Your life is out of your control and at the mercy of your anger and irrationality.

On the other side is forgiveness and a heart that recognises it wants to heal. It accepts that things happen and over time finds space for forgiveness. The empty void that appears once the blame and anger are removed by forgiveness is filled with warm, tender emotions, love and a sense of peace. This allows you to spend time remembering and honouring your furry loved one – a gift you will carry for a lifetime.

Forgiveness, and more so self-forgiveness, is such a courageous and loving thing to give yourself. It is a brave person who commits to their healing journey and seeks a resolution through the gift of forgiveness. Can you choose to be that person?

How much you can forgive others often aligns with how much you love yourself. When you truly love yourself, you won't live with bitterness and resentment running rampant within. You will be guided to forgive naturally and to remove the negative toxins of anger and non-forgiveness.

Yes, it is tricky to forgive but not impossible. Pondering the following strategies may help you change your perception and move you towards forgiveness and a calmer, more peaceful existence. Forgiving makes space for a life filled with more love.

FORGIVENESS STRATEGIES

- Think about the good qualities the person who you wish to forgive possesses. You may feel like only focusing on the negatives, but this does not help to soothe your sorrowful soul. Showing compassion and gentleness for their human misgivings can. Using affirmations such as 'They did the best they could at the time with what they knew' may help shift your perception and bring you to a more understanding place.

- Think back to a time when you made a mistake and sought forgiveness. How did you approach the person you needed forgiveness from? How did you feel when you received their forgiveness? Putting yourself in the shoes of the person needing forgiveness helps you to understand that we all make mistakes and are all human.

- Try to remember the last time you forgave someone and how this was possible. What did you do to come to this forgiveness? Is there something you did on that occasion that can help you in this situation?

- Consider if you are expecting too much from the person who you need to forgive. Are you placing them in a position that sets them up to fail? Maybe you know they do not have the capacity to live up to your expectations. Each person has a different level of emotional maturity. Accepting this and accepting people for who they are, and their limited or not limited capacities, helps us to remove judgement and introduce compassion. You may think someone's actions are a direct result of them wanting to hurt you. But most likely it has nothing to do with you and everything to do with what they are capable of. They

- 🐾 may just be trying to get through their day as best they can.
- 🐾 Check to see if your anger is misdirected. Sometimes we fire our anger at others to protect us from looking at our anger towards ourselves or the sadness buried below that anger. It is easier to be angry at someone else than ourselves. Be honest for your heart's sake.

In a nutshell, we all make mistakes; we are only human. We get to choose to eradicate the bitterness and toxins running inside us by forgiving and creating space for love and peace. Remember, this does not mean you have to have this person in your life, but it allows you to take control and release the attachment from the other person.

Empower your heart by integrating this information to find a way to forgive, learn more about yourself, move out of your comfort zone, find forgiveness in your heart and take another step towards healing your grief.

Pets forgive all the time. It's a big lesson they model to us. Think about your pet and the times you tell them off and they still sit at your feet with their enormous eyes just waiting for some more love from you. They don't hold grudges and just love unconditionally. Whatever you feel angry or guilty about, either with yourself or others, your pet would want you to shake it off. Drop, wriggle and roll it off at the park! Life is really about being peaceful, content and living fully in the moment, and to do that sometimes we just need to let it go and forgive. That is what I learnt from Max.

To move through our grief we need to forgive. Firstly stop. Recall the first ITP step, to be aware of what is swilling around inside. Then take the second ITP step, to take responsibility. The third step is to feel the emotions as you immerse yourself in them. Now you learn about forgiveness as the fourth step. These all help you to process and move through your grief.

Pink Pet Reflections: Forgiveness

Stop, take a deep breath and reflect. Give yourself permission to go inward, access your Inner Pink Star and the paw prints on your heart. Follow their lead all the way home to the pure, unconditional love of two souls connected as one, holding a love that never dies as you heal your loss, feel the love and appreciate the lessons, knowing that *the whole point is love!*

Honour yourself and your pet as you ponder the questions below that walk you to forgiveness. Record your feelings in your Pink Pet Grief Journal.

- Do I see forgiveness as a gift? Is it an opportunity for inner freedom?
- Do I believe I deserve forgiveness? If not, why not?
- Am I willing to forgive myself and/or others?
- How would my life improve if I could forgive?
- Do I have the willingness and courage to find forgiveness?

After you have pondered these questions, taking just one step at a time, see if you are a little closer to the gift of forgiveness. Review the words and the feelings and take some time out for yourself. Do not be surprised if the gift of forgiveness brings with it healing tears. It is a monumental gift of love to yourself. Be proud of yourself for receiving it. Well done!

In The Pink Process Step 5: Acceptance

As you allow forgiveness to wash over you, you can move on to the last step of the ITP Process, *acceptance*, which walks you to your new life. Forgiveness led me to a higher appreciation of my heart and soul and finally to an acceptance of my new reality – the fifth and final ITP step. I was still grieving but had acceptance. I had survived the worst of it and was able to accept my new life without Max by my side. I could find the gratitude for Max, our lives together, the lessons he gifted me, and the whole experience of life with all its twists and turns. Acceptance walks you to your new life.

Acceptance brings a loving kind of inner light. At this stage, when you arrive at acceptance, you are likely to have moved through the nasty grief attacks and emotions and have settled into a space where you understand what has happened. You accept this is now your new reality.

Once I had gained acceptance, I knew I could now cope with whatever grief threw at me and that despite the difficultness of this, I was injected with an intense, deep-seated yearning to welcome more furry souls into my life in honour of my Max. I wanted to give them a warm, loving and safe home and bed – normally mine. This had me welcoming a new furry family member to my heart and my home only a few months after I arrived at this stage of my grief journey.

Moving into the stage of acceptance does not mean you will stop crying streams of tears. It does not mean you are happy about life without your little friend. It does not mean you don't want things as they were, and it does not mean everything is rosy. What it means is that you have accepted your reality and things feel real again, even though it isn't necessarily a nice real. You will have awareness of and understand your feelings, thoughts and behaviours and how to look after yourself as you continue through your grief journey.

Loving Grief Models

You have had time to allow the grief to wash over your soul, bringing both love and devastation. You have allowed yourself to think about and feel your grief. You have found awareness, taken responsibility, felt your feelings and found forgiveness. You have honoured and thought much about your furry loved one. You will have gained some clarity around their death and any ponderings about life and mortality, maybe your own or just in general, that have arisen because of your loss.

Your acceptance can bring clarity around your situation and with it an inner calm, helping you to stop resisting and fighting your grief. You may still swing back to the other stages, but life is starting to get a little easier and you recognise your world once again.

Acceptance brings clarity and calm.

In taking time to think about acceptance and your journey, you can make good use of the lessons about yourself and the grief journey as you move on without your precious pet at your heels. You now have an opportunity to review, redesign and redecorate your life, or maybe welcome another pet into your world. Anything is possible when you have acceptance. It means you are nearing the latter part of the grief journey and can walk forward with more ease.

You find acceptance in living in the present moment and fully acknowledging your loss. You no longer live in denial and are present in the acceptance phase of grief despite still mourning your furry loved one. You have taken responsibility for your life, your loss and your actions. Once responsibility is found acceptance is not far behind.

At the acceptance stage you will feel healthier. You will have more energy and your mind will feel freer to think and do other things besides living with grief. You will start to slowly assimilate into your world again, albeit a different one.

Loss, Love and Lessons

It took me many months to reach the acceptance stage, but I knew when I had because life became brighter. There was more space between the grief attacks and fewer tears. A little part of me felt warm and glowing, and my heart and soul were tiptoeing lightly through my body rather than trudging. I became a little excited and started researching another fur child.

I was emerging from my grief haze as I began to release the veil of protection that I had been using to keep me safe. I was opening up to others and didn't feel everything was a sad event. I focused again on the positives before the negatives and the good before the bad. I stopped anticipating the worst at every corner.

I stopped worrying that if I added another furry family member I would just get hurt again. Realistically, I knew I would be hurt again – we generally outlive our animals – but I had learnt I can cope with this. The unconditional love was worth the deep heartache. This made me want to give and receive more love than ever before to more furry souls. There were so many out there looking for a good home, and I had one to give.

I changed through the grief journey. I was becoming more connected to myself and allowing my vulnerabilities and softer side to shine through. I truly believed I could cope with anything once I had arrived at this part in my journey.

Regardless of how much it had hurt to lose Max, I learnt that the hurt was worth every ounce of the love. Without the hurt there would have been no love. I was going to open myself up again for as much love as I could muster without fearing the losses. They would come again. But when they did, I would be better equipped to deal with them, and I would be more self-loving to allow the grief journey to take place whenever it needed to.

My heart has become more tender and sensitive to its surroundings, in a good way. This tender side is full of admiration for life. I have become more loving and connected to myself. I continue to think and remember Max. In a way, he lives in me. The unconditional love he gave me during his short stay here remains in my heart. He gifted me this lesson that is now entrenched deeply within.

Once you do have acceptance your life will begin to change. If you have flushed out the grief and followed your journey authentically, you will feel light and uplifted. Maybe you are beginning to let grief heal you rather than obstruct you, and maybe you are nearing the time to add to your family once again.

This takes us through the five steps. Use the ITP Process steps to gently rebuild yourself emotionally through your grief journey as you integrate grief fully. You now know the value of the first ITP step, to be aware of what emotions are swirling within you. In taking the second ITP step, you take responsibility for all that is occurring within you in your grief. No avoidance. The third step is to feel the emotions you are now aware of and to take responsibility for them as you immerse yourself in them. The fourth step is to seek forgiveness. Finally, you accept your new reality, which includes accepting whatever grief throws your way. All steps guide you through your grief journey. Remember throughout to be loving and gentle with yourself. Your pet would want that.

Pink Pet Reflections: Acceptance

Stop, take a deep breath and reflect. Give yourself permission to go inward, access your Inner Pink Star and the paw prints on your heart. Follow their lead all the way home to the pure, unconditional love of two souls connected as one, holding a love that never dies as you heal your loss, feel the love and appreciate the lessons, knowing that *the whole point is love!*

Review and ponder the questions below that may help you move towards acceptance. Answer the questions as you honour yourself and your pet. Record your feelings in your Pink Pet Grief Journal.

- Can I accept my new reality?
- Am I willing to accept my new reality?
- If so, does acceptance change how I feel?
- What is the most difficult thing about acceptance?
- What is different about myself now that I have reached acceptance?

Ponder your answers and see how you feel about your new reality. Are you nearing acceptance? Acceptance is not an easy step and can take some time to reach. Be gentle and take some time out for yourself.

Pink Pet Love Note

Everyone I have spoken to about your passing has fallen into a cloud of tears, even people who do not normally show emotion. You touched so many Max; it's the unconditional love you gift outwards that touches the unconditional love in our hearts, causing tears of grief and love to spill over…

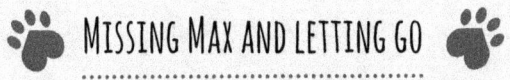 MISSING MAX AND LETTING GO

I missed Max and was grappling with coming to terms of all the stages and phases of grief. I had a deep longing for him and a profound sense of loss that felt like a bottomless pit. I was holding on tightly to the grief, believing that if I let go of it I would let go of Max. If I moved forward, I felt I would be leaving him behind. I couldn't shake these feelings.

When I collected the urn I felt disbelief. To think his ashes were in there was implausible. My big beautiful Max compacted to this small urn. Even though the urn was presented beautifully in a black felt bag with a gold drawstring, its beauty did not distract me even slightly from feeling devastated. Having him back with me was a comfort, and I carried him like the most precious cargo. When I arrived home, I gently placed him on the kitchen table and placed his boots next to his urn. Lord Max was home to occupy the seat of his throne at his shrine. His shrine was complete. A kitchen table filled with him and his life.

I often sat at his shrine for hours processing, remembering, expressing and just being with my grief as I journeyed through my grief as it asked. For a long time, I remained in the cycle of grief experiencing the rainbow of emotions while following the paw prints – waiting for the day I would be granted some respite. Much later, I would realise that I could let go of the grief and move forward while still retaining my love for Max.

Loss, Love and Lessons

Pink Pet Love Note

Take care, baby boy. Raise hell at Rainbow Bridge, and don't forget us. We love you to the moon and back, one million times over...

Love and Grief Tools and Strategies

"He is your friend, your partner, your defender, your dog. You are his life, his love, his leader. He will be yours, faithful and true, to the last beat of his heart. You owe it to him to be worthy of such devotion."

—Unknown

There are countless tools, strategies and activities you can delve into to help you to feel, process, express and heal your grief. Not every tool will work for you; some will and some won't. Some you may not even be aware of. Each person has their own individual grief journey and, as we are all so different, you need to find what works for you. Search high and low to find the strategies or tools that open your heart to heal.

It's a good idea to try different things, maybe even things outside your comfort zone. Explore, play and be curious. See what settles on your heart and brings some respite and healing to your sorrow. Grief can take you right out of your comfort zone. So, it makes sense then that you may need to try tools that you have never thought of using before to process your grief.

Loss, Love and Lessons

Below is an extensive list of tools and strategies you can consider as you walk the grief journey. Many are interchangeable between any of your losses, with some specifically related to pet grief. Many activities are more creative and internal in nature, such as arts and crafts, writing/journalling, and self-love through cooking or bubble baths! Some are more external, though obviously with an internal impact, such as yoga, exercise, going to the movies, reading relevant blogs, listening to podcasts and consulting a psychologist or grief counsellor. There is a myriad of options out there to help you process and heal your pet loss.

Further on in this chapter, I share in more depth the three main types of internal or creative activity or tools that have been invaluable in my grief journeys and in life: the arts, yoga and meditation.

In deciding what you should try, you will find my 'Calling on Your Inner Pink Star' process helpful. It's about listening in to your own inner GPS, which knows you best.

It is hard to ask for help. I struggled at first too. But at some point, you may need to acknowledge that you have done all you can on your own and that you need some external or professional help to assist you to heal and move on with your life. It is easy to get stuck in grief or feel like you are drowning among the rainbow of grief emotions with no way out. Maybe it's at this stage you can look outwards and see what is available.

It is a sign of courage, not weakness to ask for help. Sharing your story helps to process the grief. Sitting with someone who is non-judgemental and allows you to retell your story many times brings a sense of safety. This safety can allow you to face your grief. It can enable you to go deep in your heart and feel the loss.

Engaging with a community that is in a similar situation to you can also encourage you to open up and share while feeling like you belong. This is especially helpful when you feel very alone through your grief. Since pet grief can isolate you even more, the feeling of being surrounded by other pet lovers who appreciate the depth of your loss reassures you that your grief is valid and necessary to your healing.

Whether you decide to do some inner work or an external activity, go gently and slowly and only do so much at one time. Don't try to do it all at once as this will only add more stress to your already fragile soul and overwhelm you. You need time to rest also. Listen with awareness to what your inner self tells you.

One day at a time, one tool at a time, one reflection at a time to see what is right for you.

Pink Pet Love Note

Max, I see your face in my mind and it brings me joy: the big sunglass marks that developed around your eyes as you aged, your big clown smile, the floppy ears as you trotted down the hallway. Your exquisite inner and outer beauty only deepened the older you got...

Your love-grief toolbox

"A boy can learn a lot from a dog: obedience, loyalty and the importance of turning around three times before lying down."

—Robert Benchley

There are a myriad of tools and strategies that you and your Inner Creator can undertake to support you through the stages of grief. Use the Calling on Your Inner Pink Star Process at any time to direct you to your Inner Creator and choose the tools that may be right for you from the extensive list below.

I have separated the ideas into different categories. See which ones you are attracted to and just start with one. As you proceed with each activity notice how your grief feels, what the grief wants you to do and what your grief is teaching you.

WRITING

- Share your story through the written word. Detail the events leading up to your pet's passing, the actual passing and following the passing.
- Journal your thoughts and feelings to help find clarity.
- Diarise all the events you can remember that included your pet and all the funny, quirky and loving antics that made your pet who they were.
- Write a love letter to your pet.
- Write some poetry about your pet or your feelings.
- Write a eulogy for your pet for a memorial ceremony.
- Write some music.
- Write a thank-you card to anyone who has shown you support such as the vet, your friends or your family.
- Write a book.

ARTS AND CRAFTS

- Make a photo album, computer collage or online bound book, scatter individual photos in frames around the house and print some photos for the wall.
- Scrapbook memorabilia that reminds you of your pet.
- Paint on canvas or draw on paper.
- Commission a painting.
- Express with crayons, pencils, pens or paints in any form.
- Commission a piece of art.
- Make a sculpture or pottery piece.

Love and Grief Tools and Strategies

- Play with paper mache to create a piece.
- Make a quilt, sew or knit.
- Create a memory jar – write memories on a piece of paper and place them in the jar.
- Make a metalwork piece.
- Create a memory box for all your pet's items.
- Create a tribute to your pet, eg. a letter or book.
- Purchase or make a special ornament or Christmas decoration.
- Make or commission a special jewellery piece.
- Burn or make some candles.
- Try burning different essential oils.
- Make a DVD of your pet.
- Children especially may like to make puppets, give a puppet show or make a paw print or card.

OUTDOORS

- Plant a tree.
- Spend time in the garden.
- Pot some plants or flowers.
- Arrange some flowers.
- Create a pot plant with your pet's collar around it.
- Paint a mural (or get one painted) of your pets on your outdoor wall.
- Buy and paint a special bench for the garden.
- Get a stone from their special park for the garden.
- Dedicate an area in the garden for them.
- Engrave a stone for them.

MOVEMENT

- Earth yourself with daily walks along the beach or around the suburbs or barefoot in the park.
- Run on the treadmill or around the streets.
- Visit the gym and use the weights and treadmill or join a class.
- Practise yoga, meditation, tai chi, Pilates, chanting or breath exercises.
- Dance – any kind.
- Get moving – any kind of movement.
- Have fun with water activities, eg. swimming, surfing, snorkelling, diving, stand up paddle board, kite surfing.
- Declutter your house.
- Build a sandcastle at the beach.

MUSIC

- Play or learn a musical instrument.
- Listen to music.
- Create playlists that soothe the soul on, for example, Spotify, iTunes or Sound Cloud.
- Visit the theatre.
- Go to a concert.
- Design your own concert.
- Make a CD.

SOCIAL

- Host a doggy park party to thank all your park friends for being supportive.

Love and Grief Tools and Strategies

- Reach out to others who have lost their pets and acknowledge their grief.
- Hug other pets.
- Take up a new hobby.
- Go to the movies.
- Have coffee with friends.
- Take classes with friends.
- Learn a new language.
- Travel or take a holiday.
- Go window shopping.

SELF-LOVE

- Read all the books that call out to you.
- Sign up to online newsletters in your area of interest.
- Create an altar in your house with all your pet's special things.
- Cook a scrumptious dinner.
- Get beautiful massages.
- Spend time at home just being.
- Have a bubble bath.
- Take a daytime nap.
- Change to a healthy diet.
- Drink less alcohol and/or decide to give up any other bad habits or addictions.
- Find a special place for your pet's lead and collar and take time to spend with their belongings.

EXTERNAL SUPPORT

- Visit a psychologist, counsellor or life coach who specialises in pet grief.
- Read literature on grief, expressly pet grief.
- Read pet loss poems or quotes.
- Join relevant websites newsletter lists.
- Read blog posts on pet grief.
- Listen to podcasts or YouTube videos on pet grief.
- Join social media pages on pet grief.
- Post memorial tributes on websites.
- Join an animal association or volunteer your time.
- Foster an animal.
- Help other pets that need assistance, eg. knitting jumpers for lambs without mothers or other initiatives.
- Donate to an animal organisation or charity.
- See the *Other helpful links* at the end of this book.

Now let's take a closer look at a few tools and strategies that I particularly love and utilise: the arts, yoga and meditation.

♥ PINK PET LOVE NOTE ♥

I look back on our memories and they are all iced in fun, laughter, adventures but most of all devotion and love. How lucky am I?...

Love and Grief Tools and Strategies

The Arts

"Everything I know, I learnt from dogs."

—Nora Roberts

Are you a delightful painter, an elegant dancer, an ice skating extraordinaire or a prolific writer and you just don't know it yet? Or do you dabble and, while you are no Leonardo DaVinci, for you it is cathartic, freeing and liberating... and that is what matters most? As each brush stroke is laid on a blank canvas or as each word unravels itself gently on the page, you may be a tiny bit closer to healing your grief.

My first book *Heartbreak, Healing and Happiness* came to fruition straight out of a very painful event in my life. At school I never got anything better than a C for my essays. I labelled myself as 'not a writer' and 'not creative'. In hindsight, I built my life around a great untruth. When my heartbreak occurred, I sat at the computer and the words flooded out of my heart through my fingers to the pages in front of me. I quickly finished my 80,000-word manuscript, almost without flinching. I felt like a channel for something bigger.

My heart surely knew what it wanted to say and my head stayed quiet for once. Writing became my channel, my saviour. Later it became my life and business. Little did I know many years prior that I was to become an author. I had always had a pipedream to write a book, but I don't think I believed I would really do it. Since then I have written my second book *Grief, Grace and Gratitude* in honour of my father's passing and now this book, my third, in honour of the loss of Max.

Follow the whisper and the paw prints on your heart.

Loss, Love and Lessons

Each book has walked me through my grief and helped heal the pain. Each time I wrote 'The End', I had felt my grief, processed it, expressed it and healed it. I did this while also sharing my experience, professional knowledge and life lessons to help other vulnerable souls on a similar journey. I knew that by reading my books, others could begin to feel not so alone and learn new skills as they start to believe they also can heal.

We all go through pain – some more than others. If we look around, some of our planet's most creative souls have suffered through deep and dark pain. These sensitive individuals use their craft to work through and heal their emotions, and we get to benefit from the beauty of their artistry expressed in music, dance or theatre. You may notice that the more pain someone is in, it seems the better they are at what they do and the more committed they are. Their expressive work becomes their therapy. Think of the famous impressionist painter Vincent Van Gogh or the beautiful Persian poet Rumi.

I definitely don't wish you added pain simply to turn you into a famous artist! However, I wish for you to understand that no matter where you sit with your pain, the gift of your Inner Creator lies deep within you, waiting to be unleashed. Your heart is beckoning you to take the plunge deep within and offers to assist you to move you through your suffering. Given the right environment, your heart has the ability to heal. Going inwards is the first step to building the environment for that to occur.

It takes wisdom to know what your special talent or craft is. I can't imagine Elton John would have been a great ice skater or that Rumi would have pumped out songs like Pink, the American singer-songwriter. They found the perfect artistic craft for their personal self-expression. The craft for you is not necessarily one that makes you famous but the one that acts like therapy. It soothes your soul in a nurturing and nourishing environment.

In that safe space your grief can surface. It's like someone reaches deep inside you and pulls your grief through you and places it on

Love and Grief Tools and Strategies

the cusp of your heart. From there you can access it and begin to process it, moving the energy through you in the form of anger, sadness, anxiety, depression and all the other emotions that grief arrives with.

If you are lucky you may find more than one talent or craft. One of the most special things I created with the help of a professional painter was a mural on my outside wall in the dog feeding area. It depicts a life-size portrait of Max, Suzy and Chelsea (a black senior Labrador I rescued about eighteen months after Max passed away) surrounded by flowers and butterflies with a chandelier above them. All symbols from my books. Every night, I go to feed Suzy and Chelsea and sit and admire my mural, remembering Max with smiles and sometimes chuckles.

Before completing my second book, I also turned to yoga to help nourish, nurture and heal my mind, body and spirit. I learnt to sit with my feelings better and reduce my stress, dropping the masks that hid my true self and meeting myself intimately while balancing my whole being. I soon fell totally in love with yoga and have since completed the first two levels of yoga teacher training.

Neither of these paths would have come to fruition in my life if it wasn't for my grief and my heartbreak, and for that I am thankful. You just need to listen to your heart and it will tell you where to go next. It helps to be open to variety. Try new things and see how they resonate with you. Find your Inner Creator and what it likes. Find inner joy when you unlock the deep inner space that is filled with your beauty and delights. This will begin to cleanse and release you from the suffering of your grief.

Grief can initiate the revealing of your gifts and talents as you connect with your Inner Creator and follow the paw prints on your heart to your favourite form of self-expression. This may not only profoundly transform your inner self and grief but maybe your career

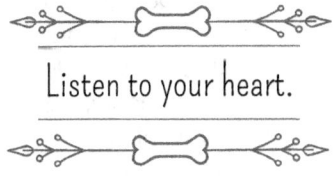

Listen to your heart.

and even your entire life. It can potentially unleash your deepest passions and life purpose.

You know which craft is working because when it draws the grief to the surface to process, there may be a bittersweet feeling – a sense of joy at your self-expression but also a sense of sorrow from the hurt. Underneath that hurt will be a rippling energy that highlights your inner knowing that you are on the right path to healing your grief.

> ### 🐾 Pink Pet Love Note 🐾
>
> I am so grateful for having had you in my life, Max. You taught me so much. The gifts you left behind are endless. You were here for too short a time, but you live in my heart every day...

Yoga

"My little dog – a heartbeat at my feet."

—Edith Wharton

As mentioned, I found yoga to be a beautiful gift. This remarkable tool can instigate profound change and healing, helping you through your grief. The ancient tradition of yoga is over 5000 years old and means different things to different people. At its core, it is a non-judgemental practice that is based on kindness and wishes happiness and an inner connectedness for all beings. It respects the sacred nature of life.

Love and Grief Tools and Strategies

If yoga is a foreign concept for you, and you feel a little resistant, just take what resonates here and leave the rest. I do encourage you though that glimpsing outside your comfort zone to learn new strategies can be eye-opening. The more info you are armed with the better.

If yoga has piqued your interest previously, perhaps now is the time to give it a go. If you are already deep into yoga and know firsthand the aliveness, joyfulness and peace it can bring, you may be encouraged to solidify your practice even further to assist you on the grief journey.

Yoga means union, to bring together the body, mind and spirit. The yoga goal is to bring about the cessation of suffering and have us arrive at our natural state, which drops away the small self or the ego, purifies the mind and allows our true identity and natural state to awaken. It allows us, like children, to be immersed in our naturalness. Yoga gives us awareness of consciousness to be able to find this sacred space internally.

Through a state of awareness, yoga allows us to connect with our blissful nature, our essential being, that lives in ecstatic love, peace and joy, regardless of what is happening around us. Yoga can take us through postures (Asana) to achieve strength, flexibility, balance, alignment and tone, breath work (Pranayama) to calm the sympathetic nervous system and meditation (Dhyana) to help silence the fluctuations of the mind. Other forms of yoga may include chanting, intentions and dedications, philosophy, restorative and deep relaxation (Yoga Nidra).

Many of us spend a lifetime seeking wholeness and happiness. We yearn inner peace and joy and mostly seek this outside of ourselves, hoping to fill the empty void with all sorts of healthy or unhealthy ways: another house, another job, another child, another new outfit, a swimming pool, a new gym membership, another dinner party, another friend, another exciting or drama-filled event. We still feel something is missing. We feel unhappy, alone or just empty. At some point, we may realise the external world is not providing the answers and yet we continue to battle, often because we know no different.

Sometimes it is this realisation that can in turn bring us to yoga and the start of a lifetime journey within. We want to heal so we try something different to unearth an inward connection with ourselves, seeking inner peace. We know it is not attainable through the external world in our material society, so we must go inwards. There is no other way. However, learning to run towards ourselves instead of away from ourselves can be terrifying when we are drowning in grief emotions.

Yoga says that we are all whole and this is always inherently inside each one of us. We simply need to remove the outward suffering, ego and mind chitter chatter to be able to see what is already inside us and reconnect to that blissful place. This will bring about everything we are looking for.

It is not about changing ourselves but more about returning home to our true and pure nature that has always resided deep within.

Yoga helped transform my stress levels, health, sleep, hormones, Type A personality, perfectionism, people-pleasing, ability to say no, ability to sit with myself, desire to remove drama from my life and my ability to grieve healthily. It helped me to find my purpose, eat better, drink less, improve how I thought about myself and the list goes on. I had been on a spiritual and seeking journey for a long time yet once I found yoga it was amplified tenfold. Joy, peace and inner happiness became my most natural state.

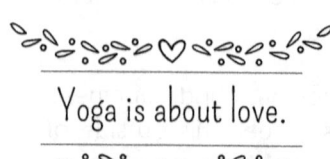
Yoga is about love.

Yoga is beneficial to grief mainly because you meet yourself inwardly and learn to sit with your emotions. By sitting with your emotions, their energy rises to the surface to be honoured and felt. The trickiest part of grief in the Western world, I believe, is the ability to sit with your emotions. You run, you hide,

Love and Grief Tools and Strategies

you distract yourself. You do whatever it takes to avoid, repress and suppress, and then you pay for this because you end up with depression, anxiety, addictions or other internal issues.

You are told to get over it, to not cry. Ignore it and run away fast. What people *should* be saying is to cry your eyes out, get it out, yell, scream, shake. Do whatever you need to do to purge the grief, without hurting anyone. There will always be an element of grief assimilated within you that you carry around, but I'm talking about clearing the intense initial grief that halts your life. That's what you need to process first.

Yoga provided a sweet haven to process my grief in, and it may for you too. This led me to all the love buried below the rainbow of grief emotions. Things began to make sense as the bigger questions in my mind were getting answered. Most of the insecurities that I carried along the way fell into my wake. The grief rose and I met it head on. I had found the connection to myself and I didn't need to wear a mask any longer. I cared for and nurtured myself like I cared for Max, full of love.

Suddenly everything made sense. Once I was able to sit still long enough to be with my heart, beautiful things happened. I found a strong inner connection to my heart that walked me to honour and respect myself at every level. I experienced a warm and fuzzy sense of joy, realising that *the whole point is love!* I knew that having found the love inside, I could sense it everywhere. I also understood that without grief there is no love. So to have grief in my life at such a deep level meant I had, and still have, such deep love. I was grateful for that.

The love was worth all the pain I had to manoeuvre myself through.

When you go through grief and heal in a healthy fashion, you know that if you ever go through it again, you will cope. So, life and death do not scare you as much. You love your heart out and know that when grief knocks at your door, you will answer and follow its lead. In the meantime, you will avoid nothing in fear of grief. Hence, you get to love so much more and not live small or on guard for grief to take hold again. You just live and love.

I encourage you to sit with your feelings and be good with that. It just is what it is. No emotion is permanent, so learn to sit and let the physical and emotional grief emotion rise through your body. Allow this to happen without attaching or judging the myriad of thoughts that arrive to try to take you down a rabbit hole of confusion and depression. Continue to sit with all that is. This is the key to moving through your grief. That is why yoga is so beautifully effective and a gorgeous gift.

You also need to be mindful that if you ever feel really stuck, you may need to ask for help. You will most likely feel the difference if you arrive at this point. Trust your judgement. If it feels like you can't cope, ask for help. Support is always there; you just need to find what works for you.

So, if it is that your ears are pricked and you are interested in pursuing yoga to aid in processing and healing your grief, do your research. Check out your local area and go along to a class. Speak with likeminded friends and get some recommendations.

There are many different styles of yoga that can be held in homes, studios and even gyms. Some are more physical and some more spiritual. Some teachers are enlightening, some not so much. Try different styles and see which best fits you. Speak with the instructor and ensure that you feel comfortable with their way of teaching and that their values align with your own. You will know by how you feel.

No judgement, no attachment.

Remember, just do what is right for you right now. Maybe, however, this is not for you and that's perfectly okay too.

Just follow the paw prints on your heart and allow them to lead the way.

LOVE AND GRIEF TOOLS AND STRATEGIES

BENEFITS OF YOGA

- unites, nourishes, nurtures and heals the body, mind and heart
- provides flexibility, balance, strength, alignment and tone
- loosens the tension in the body and mind
- allows us to analyse less, feel more and breathe more as we sit with our feelings, inviting self-enquiry
- shows us kindness and compassion and to treat our mind, body and heart with more love and care
- provides an understanding that every emotion is temporary
- activates the parasympathetic nervous system, calming the body
- allows you to surrender to what is in this present moment
- boosts self-esteem and confidence while cultivating happiness and joy
- improves your mood
- promotes self-awareness, self-esteem, self-confidence and self-acceptance
- encourages joy and happiness
- brings awareness and clarity
- improves respiration, metabolism, digestion, vitality, lymphatic system, immune system, blood pressure, blood flow, sleep, pain, tension, adrenal glands and stress
- nurtures your muscles, bones, joints, cartilage, spine
- brings beauty to your life.

> ### 🐾 Pink Pet Love Note 🐾
>
> You taught me how to love a million times over. You taught me how to find the love entrenched deep in my heart...

Meditation

> *"Keep calm and pat a dog."*
>
> —Unknown

Meditation is part of the yoga tradition, but you can choose to meditate without practising yoga. Alternatively, you can practise meditation while in a yoga Asana or even while walking. Like yoga, meditation has numerous benefits and is becoming an increasingly popular tool in the West to help still busy minds in our chaotic world. Adding grief to your already busy world puts added pressure on your mind and can send you into emotional overwhelm. So a tool such as meditation is definitely worth a try.

Essentially, meditation provides you with an opportunity to train, quieten and soften your mind. You focus on what is happening and what you are sensing in the body rather than focusing on the thoughts racing around in your head. As the mind settles, you can connect with your true self that lies under the mind's chitter chatter. The mind, body and heart can begin to unite and function in harmony, bringing you to a place of connection and balance, allowing you to find a calmer and more stable state. You will slowly realise that all the suffering you experience is from the busy mind chatter and that beyond that is a blissful, natural state.

Love and Grief Tools and Strategies

Meditation helps you to avoid the emotional traps and in turn improve your mental and emotional health, which leads to a more peaceful and joyful life. Once you realise you can take some control back and change how you react to the mind's incessant noise, you can find internal freedom – an empowering and enlightening space to live life differently. This is the oasis of peace that is deep within and the beautiful space that you can begin to heal from your suffering and grief.

Meditation teaches you to observe and be aware of what is happening in the mind and the body. To feel all the sensations of the inner world. To let go and surrender to the endless stream of thoughts. To sit back from your busy mind and just watch with awareness while you feel the experience and allow the clarity and spacious stillness to envelop you. Soon after, be reassured that the blissful state can appear. Meditation does not have to be perfect. You only need to do a little every day and build up over time.

Mindfulness plays a part in meditation, as it does in yoga. Mindfulness is identified as being in a state where your attention is fully on the present. The focal point of your meditation will be either your breath or a mantra, where you repeat a sound or word that has special meaning to you. Thoughts will still naturally arise. Meditation is the practice of becoming aware of those thoughts through mindfulness, acknowledging them and then letting them go without judgement or attachment. You then return to the breath or the mantra.

Thoughts are like the clouds in the sky and observing the sky is like observing the self. Your thoughts and feelings are like the weather. The weather comes and goes, in a constant state of flux in all forms of storms, hurricanes, tsunamis and torrential rains. Yet none of these alters the sky above it all. The beautiful blue sky waits for all the activity to pass, always patient, strong, reliable, serene and peaceful. It always passes because nothing is permanent.

So when we look at the sky and we see only clouds it's like seeing our thoughts when we look into our mind. Beyond the thoughts lies a beautiful self that is calm, joyful and peaceful, waiting for the tirade of thoughts to pass or for us to not attach to the thought patterns that emerge.

Another way to look at them is to think of the sea. If you have been scuba diving, you may relate to this one a bit deeper. On the top of the sea, you can have storms, tidal waves, ten-metre swells and absolute chaos. At the bottom of the deep sea, however, there may be a slight sway of the water body and its surrounding plant life. Yet it sits strong and waits for the pandemonium above to pass.

Similarly, deep inside you is this strong and still place that is unwavering and grounded. If you operate from this heart space, all the pain that rains over you can be dealt with. Your thoughts and emotions come in waves and you simply need to allow them to pass. While you wait, if you don't attach to the thoughts and instead allow them to ride through you, you go back to operate from your deeper self and you will walk much more easily through the pain and arrive back, grounded and peaceful.

Thoughts are thoughts and they will always be there. It is the motion of us chasing them down the rabbit hole that causes us so much stress. It is then the avoidance of this pain that causes us so much suffering. Just let the thoughts and emotions be. They will pass, and then your clarity and peace deep within will reappear.

With meditation it's better to let go of the theory and just jump in. There are many apps available to download that will walk you through guided meditations and deep relaxations. (Four are mentioned in the *Other helpful links* section at the end of the book.) Choosing an app is a very personal choice, so if you just search for 'meditation' in the app store, you can take a look at the individual apps and see which appeal to you.

There are many meditation scripts available on the internet and in other books. I have included two of my own in the *Appendix* at the

Love and Grief Tools and Strategies

back of this book for you to try: a shorter one to get started and a longer version for when you are ready to delve a little deeper.

During meditation, many find it difficult to sit still and not fidget or think about what's for dinner. Others struggle because it highlights their biggest fears and emotions as they rise to the surface to be dealt with. Yoga and meditation are big revealers, highlighting to us where we may be stuck. It can take some courage to delve into your inner world, but the practice begets magnificent rewards if done regularly.

I love saying mantras in my meditation and yoga practice, finding it focuses my mind and brings me inner balance and wellbeing. Mantras are as easy as sitting comfortably, closing your eyes and repeating the words over and over. 'Lokah Samastah Sukhino Bhavantu' is one of my favourite powerful Sanskrit mantras. It assists us in our spiritual evolution and acts as a blessing for the world. It translates to mean 'May all beings everywhere be happy and free, and may the thoughts, words and actions of my own life contribute in some way to that happiness and to that freedom for all'.

I love this mantra as it relates to all beings. I envisage this encapsulating not only humans but all animals: dogs, cats, elephants, bears, lizards, millipedes, stick insects, birds, giraffes, penguins and so on.

BENEFITS OF MEDITATION

- reduces stress, loneliness, fear, depression and anxiety
- settles thoughts and emotions while building emotional health and intelligence
- brings you to the present moment
- promotes self-awareness, self-esteem, self-confidence and self-acceptance

Loss, Love and Lessons

- 🐾 builds kindness, compassion, happiness and general wellbeing
- 🐾 increases vitality, focus, memory, attention span, mood, optimism and relaxation
- 🐾 improves breathing, immune function, energy levels, sleep, and decreases blood pressure
- 🐾 helps to let go of the path and find the inner oasis of peace and calm.

Each day can be beyond difficult when you lose your pet, especially if those around you don't acknowledge the depth of your loss or are diminishing your pain. It is important to look after yourself and show yourself self-love. Following the guidance in this book to assist you along your grief journey is one big act of self-love!

Remember, self-love is the ability to be gentle and compassionate with yourself despite your grief. It is about forgiveness for yourself and others. It is about having awareness and taking care of your emotional, physical, mental and spiritual needs, becoming mindful of what you really need at this moment in time. It is about self-expression and healing and learning to love yourself.

It is important to recognise the difference between grieving and suffering. Allow yourself to grieve; it is vital to your future happiness. But don't be unkind to yourself by neglecting your grief or dismissing it to appease others. It will only create more suffering, and you don't need that.

PINK PET REFLECTIONS: TOOLS LIST

Let's now compile a big list of all the grief tools that may help you feel, process, express and start to heal your grief.

Stop, take a deep breath and reflect. Give yourself permission to go inward, access your Inner Pink Star and the paw prints on your heart. Follow their lead all the way home to the pure, unconditional love of two souls connected as one, holding a love that never dies as you heal your loss, feel the love and appreciate the lessons, knowing that *the whole point is love!*

Record your feelings in your Pink Pet Grief Journal.

- Take out a big sheet of paper and list the tools and strategies that appeal to your heart and your healing. Use the Calling on Your Inner Pink Star Process if necessary.
- Highlight the top ten tools.
- Shorten your list to the top five.
- Then sort the top five into your order of priority.
- Start working through your list and arranging what you need to buy or do to work with these tools.
- Journal your thoughts, feelings, emotions, fears, revelations, disappointments and grief.

Now that you have a list of grief tools you can slowly work through the ones you think may benefit you. Go at your own pace as you try the different options. You won't know what epiphanies and internal shifts you may have until you put them into practice.

> ### Pink Pet Love Note
>
> As I sit quietly with myself, I can feel your love surround and protect my heart as it begs to heal the grief yet continue to feel the deep love...

Children and grief

> *"If there is a heaven, it's certain our animals are to be there. Their lives become so interwoven with our own, it would take more than an archangel to detangle them."*
>
> —Pam Brown

How do the grief models I have shared apply to children? How do you help them to grieve? I feel that the way children develop such sincere, deep and profound bonds with their pets — and the fact that the grieving process can differ according to their age — warrants a whole section here on children and grief.

Children and their pets seem to truly get each other. A child's pet is a best friend and they are often inseparable, doing everything together. The pet becomes an integral family member and friend, providing structure and love in children's lives and teaching them many things about responsibility, care, friendship, family, grief and love. Maybe they roll around in the garden together, get up to naughty escapades, dress up with hats and scarves, and play just like children and pets are skilled at doing.

Dogs often follow children around, wagging their tail zealously while waiting for the next game. They sit in front of their mini humans, look deep into their eyes and just wait for the next piece of fun or love to be delivered. The fur child is always ready for any attention from their best friend and just wants to shower them in love. It's no wonder they develop such unbreakable, loving bonds.

Pets really do bring an amazing element to children's lives and It is no wonder that when they experience their best friend's passing, their emotions can be overpowering and sometimes frightening. A huge emptiness suddenly appears in their lives, often leaving the parents unsure of how to journey the child through their grief. In the case of a dysfunctional family, the loss can be felt even more. This is where even school counsellors would do well to understand the stages of grief to help their students through the loss of a pet or loved one.

The grief can be made worse by the fact that the loss of their pet may well be the first real loss the child has ever experienced. The grief and how it is handled can be the precedence for future grief events. In general, they should be treated carefully, sensitively, responsibly and appropriately.

How Children View and Deal with Death

Depending on their age children may ask, "When are they coming back?" This is normal and simply reflects their limited understanding of death. Generally, children under three don't understand or realise that death is permanent. They will feel the negative energy around them but think the pet will be back. From about three to five they may think death can be reversed: their pet is dead but will come back to life. This may be due to the TV characters that come back to life in cartoons. Between about five and nine they begin to understand death's permanence. After about ten years old they begin to have the full capacity to appreciate the meaning of death.

Young teenagers can be totally devastated by the loss of their pet and struggle to process the depth of their feelings. Their pets may have become just as important in their lives and routines as all the other family surrounding them. Their first memory might be of their loyal friend sitting beside their crib. The pet may have been their lifelong confidant and biggest cheerleader, often being the only set of ears that really heard their anxieties and concerns, especially during those turbulent teenage years.

We need to be mindful that children may grieve for a shorter period than adults and may seem to return to their normal happy disposition. They may even soon ask, "Can we get another pet?" The emotional pain that they experience, however, is not necessarily any less and they need help to process their grief.

Children are often a lot smarter, have considerable intuition and are more astute than we think. They are very sensitive to their feelings. Consequently, saying goodbye to their best friend is significant and should be honoured and respected. From my experience and research, I believe allowing the child to be part of the decision-making around their pet's death, and saying their own goodbyes, helps them with their grief.

Children develop sincere, deep and profound bonds with their pets.

It often helps for children to be at the vet clinic and see or meet the vet and begin to understand the process. Vets are good at speaking with the children in these instances and may help the child feel more included and more at ease. The vet may also be able to guide you as to whether the children remain present for the euthanasia or say their goodbye and wait in the reception area with a family member or a vet nurse. From my experience working in a vet clinic, I know that sometimes seeing that the pet has died, and being able to say a final goodbye, may help a child to gain closure.

Following are more things to consider in advance to ensure your children move through the grief process in a healthy fashion.

LOVE AND GRIEF TOOLS AND STRATEGIES

HOW TO HELP CHILDREN MOVE THROUGH GRIEF

- 🐾 Be honest, truthful, clear and concise.

It is best to not overload your children with information and minor details. Spend some time alone with them and explain that the pet has died and what was the cause of death. Try to avoid half-truths or euphemisms and use direct language such as 'died', 'death' and 'dead' as these help to make it very clear to them and easier to understand. Have a conversation around the permanence of death to help them to evaluate the situation.

Using statements like they have 'gone away' or 'run away' or 'been put to sleep' can be confusing and cause the child more pain. Their grief may present differently and they may wonder what will happen if they go to sleep. Will they wake up? They may wonder if they will be sent away. They may wonder each day if the pet will return as there is no finality. It's important to be very careful with children for them to process their grief appropriately and not see them plunge further into more complicated inner issues.

- 🐾 Allow them space to ask you questions and time to assimilate your answers.

Children may ask bizarre questions or draw strange pictures to try and make sense of the death and where the pet's body is now. They may worry that they caused the death somehow, so it's good to allow them to ask questions. Likewise, ask them questions that will pre-empt any concerns they have – for example, if they feel responsible for the death – and see what they are really thinking. Of course, reassure them that this is not the case. You can ask them how they would explain the situation to their friend to gauge what understanding they have. But always continue to be open and honest with them, and allow them to process their grief.

- 🐾 Allow them to feel their feelings and sit with them.

As we know, feeling your feelings is part of the healing with grief. Children are no different. If they are sad, let them cry as much as they need. Encourage them to feel their feelings and assure them it is a normal part of grief. Each tear is allowing them to process the energy of grief through their physical body. It is important that children always know they are loved and cared for during this process.

Children often don't have the vocabulary to express what they are feeling like adults do. So to process their grief, they often act out through inappropriate behaviours. They may show aggression in certain situations, become angry, start to not feel well or experience anxiety. Being aware of this and looking for signs of changed behaviour helps you to understand what they are going through and how to care for them on their grief journey. Perhaps allow them some space to act out a bit and nurture them. Seek professional help if it continues or becomes a concern.

Don't forget to let them see you express your feelings also. This helps children to know that you as an adult are also upset and you can both cry together. This helps validates their grief as you model healing behaviour.

- Keep teachers and carers informed.

Ensure you advise teachers and adults in the children's life as to what the child is going through. They can offer an understanding of any changes and behaviours that may appear, and may also be a source of further professional help.

- Allow them to tell their story in a myriad of ways.

Children often process their feelings by doing or creating. They may like to create a memorial, spend time writing, making or playing puppets, drawing about their pet or other creative ideas. The next chapter will provide more information on memorials and ways to honour the pet for both children and adults.

Love and Grief Tools and Strategies

- 🐾 Read to your children or provide reading material to help their grief.

Seeing themselves in others' stories helps children to feel not so alone and teaches them lessons in dealing with grief – much like my sharing of Max's and my own stories with you. Our vet clinic had a beautiful book called *Lifetimes* by Bryan Mellonie that explains grief, which we would lend to parents to read to their children. Another one I have found is *When Your Pet Dies: A Healing Handbook for Kids* written by Victoria Ryan and illustrated by R W Alley.

- 🐾 Spend time with the children honouring the loss of the pet.

Build tributes or memorials with your children as a further way to process their grief and honour the loss and also to teach them the importance of the pet's life. It may be advisable not to replace the pet too soon otherwise the child may think that when they lose their pet, it is of no great importance and it can easily be replaced. If they are grieving, providing a replacement pet too soon can be like a band-aid solution to grief and doesn't teach them to acknowledge, feel and process their grief.

Just like adults, if given time and the right environment, children learn how to process their loss. They learn that to lose their furry friend is very painful, but the pain does pass, and they will find happiness, joy and love again.

I don't have any children of my own, but the night I had the ashes returned I invited the family, including my six nieces, over for dinner to celebrate Max's life. I felt vulnerable as I tried to celebrate his life while my soul was raw and hurting. Suffering mixed emotions from minute to minute, trying to sustain the grief journey, honour his life and entertain the family proved quite a challenge.

Loss, Love and Lessons

That night and over the next few weeks, all my nieces continued to ask their parents and me many questions about what happened to Max, where he was and what it meant. They were struggling themselves to get their heads around it. I decided to hold a memorial in his honour. It would allow me some much-needed closure, allow the children to process some of their grief, and give us all a chance to pay respect to Max, his loss, his love and his lessons.

In the next chapter, I will share various ways to honour the love of a pet, such as hosting a memorial ceremony, creating a tribute or eulogy, and preparing a resting place and rituals. These are helpful for adults and children alike.

Pink Pet Love Note

A special friend gave me a special gift today – a Willow ornament of a young girl nursing a puppy. I felt so sad. Max, I hope the angels came to get you and you are being nurtured and cared for in the arms of your own special angel…

Honouring the Love

"Dogs are not our whole life, but they make our lives whole."

—Roger Caras

Grief is how we feel in our inner world and mourning is the external expression of the grief and sorrow – for example, through writing in our *Pink Pet Grief Journal*, speaking with others, crying, reading a eulogy at a memorial. Mourning is an important part of healing any loss and it is no different with pet loss. How you choose to mourn reflects how you are honouring your furry loved one.

Various traditions honour their lost ones differently. So much time, attention, energy and love go into arranging a funeral to bring our friends and loved ones together to share in our loss and our love.

Pet loss is no different to someone who loves their pet like a family member, though some in society don't really deem it to be so. It is not really the norm to have a pet funeral, which makes people feel embarrassed or silly for wanting to honour their pets in the same way. As time moves on it is becoming more accepted, but there needs to be much more exposure to find the level of acknowledgement we would like for our pets.

In this section you will learn more about how to effectively honour your loved one. You will delve a little deeper into these areas listed below:

1. Burial and cremation – helps you understand what happens immediately after your pet's passing and the different options available
2. Memorial ceremony – details options on how to host a ceremony or a funeral to honour your pet
3. Tributes – teaches you different ways to pay tribute to your pet, an example of this being writing a eulogy
4. Resting place – guides you to create a beautiful place where your pet rests or a place you can dedicate to their memory
5. Rituals – explores different activities you may use to remember your pet on anniversaries.

Take some time exploring each section and contemplate what is right for you as you honour your pet and yourself with care and love. Allow your heart to soften as you process some of the grief. The paw prints on your heart will help direct you to the right decisions for you at this difficult time.

Burial and cremation

Saying goodbye to your loved one means you need to make an important decision on how to look after their body in their passing. It can be an overwhelming decision especially if the death is sudden or unexpected, adding to that the many options available to you.

It is hard to make a decision when you are in emotional overwhelm, so it is sensible to know your options beforehand. The vet clinic staff will be able to assist with all your queries and explain the different options available.

If you arrive at the vet clinic knowing that you will be euthanising your pet, it is wise to have decided as a family on your options beforehand. This way, once your pet has passed, you can just leave the clinic without having to return to the reception desk and finalise matters. This is never an easy time but preparation may take away some of the stress.

Generally, you have three options:

- 🐾 *Home burial*

    In this case, the vet clinic will ensure your loved one's body is dealt with carefully and respectfully. Most likely they will be wrapped in a rug, so you can take them home with you and find an appropriate place in your garden to lay them to rest.

- 🐾 *Cremation with the ashes returned to you in an urn of your choice*

    There is a multitude of urns available in different shapes and sizes for your pet's remains. You can choose to have the urn open or closed. Open gives you the ability to scatter the ashes at a location of your choice. Closed is preferable if you would like to keep the ashes in the urn permanently. There are other options and receptacles for your pet's remains such as necklaces that hold a small amount of their remains inside, a box with a photo on top, figurines and various others. The ashes are normally returned within a week and the presentation is respectful and beautiful. These options can be quite expensive, so you will need to consider your financial situation.

- 🐾 *Cremation with the ashes not returned*

    Others opt for a cremation with no ashes returned. Our crematorium in South Australia, Australia scatters the ashes in their rose garden. This may be different with each crematorium, so you would need to ask your vet clinic.

Any option you choose will be difficult. If possible, allow yourself a little time to see what appeals to you most. Honouring your loved one's body is an important part of honouring them and essential to the grief process.

Memorial Ceremony

Conducting a memorial ceremony can allow you to mourn and may help you cope with your loss. It can move you closer towards accepting your new reality while allowing a celebration for your beloved pet's life. After all, we attend human funerals all the time. They are a sacred ritual, sometimes extremely elaborate, to honour and celebrate a life. They are filled with support, affection and love for the recently deceased.

A memorial ceremony gives you a chance to stand still and contemplate your loss. This can be so beneficial especially when you are in shock and immersed in your loss. It brings your friends, family and support group together to provide comfort. It is one more step in the grieving process that can help you feel, process, express and start to heal your grief. It is a chance to say a proper and honourable goodbye to your furry family member. It also provides a chance to share tributes such as a eulogy with those surrounding and supporting you.

You may contemplate what others will think about having a memorial for a dog or other pet. I did, momentarily. I quickly reminded myself that this was Max, my fur angel, my child, and he deserved a great send-off. I also deserved to honour his love, and so do you! It is not about what others will think but how you want to honour your pet's life and process your emotions. So don't waste your energy on those sorts of unhealthy thought patterns. Choose to believe in yourself and move forward to plan your memorial, tributes and precious resting place for your furry loved one.

Like any funeral, organising a pet memorial can take time and the details of how you would like to hold your memorial are individual to you. There are so many ways you can plan your memorial. You may arrange a ceremony at home, in a park, on the beach, a church, at a restaurant or any place that feels special to you and your pet. Like a human funeral, the options are only limited by your imagination as to how you would like to proceed, where you will hold it and what you will include as part of the ceremony.

You may wish to include in your memorial service a eulogy, which is a type of tribute that I discuss further on in this section, other speakers, candles, poems, music, flowers, meditations, special items that belonged to your pet, refreshments – basically anything you can think of that appeals to you and helps you to process your loss.

Contemplate your loss.

Let me share with you now my story of honouring Max...

Honouring Max

I utilised a lot of the tools shared in the previous chapter as I prepared for Max's upcoming memorial, a way to honour the love. I was looking forward to the day as it approached yet I was still buried deep in my grief. It seemed never-ending. Each night I continued to sit at my kitchen table that was covered in Lord Max's shrine. He was all around me, imbedded in my heart yet so far away. I was confused by my entangled feelings. My heart and mind were all over the place trying to come to terms with the grief experience and the range of emotions that blanketed me and had me living in a hazy half-life.

I knew the memorial was going to be beautiful but was doubtful it would bring as much respite as I desired from the onslaught of emotions. I could only hope it would. Something inside me kept moving me forward with the preparations.

I wrote a special piece of prose as my eulogy for the memorial titled 'My Golden Light' (which I share at the end of this chapter) that expressed all I could of my love for him. Writing this eulogy had me in knots and almost unable to breathe as my emotions caught in my throat and my heart began to spill over once again. The words came flowing out of me as did a river of tears, all landing softly on the page, forming a perfectly created expression of all that I wanted to say.

I wrote and wrote and refined it over a few days. Each time I expressed what I felt I observed little pieces inside shifting. Sometimes it shifted to more tears and other times it was just the love. Both types of shift indicated to me I was following the paw prints that were leading me through the deep grief and hopefully out the other side. Which they did much later!

Two days before Max's memorial was his birthday. He would have been fifteen. This day was challenging. I had promised Max I would make him cupcakes for his fourteenth birthday and it didn't happen. So I had double promised for his fifteenth. But here we were, only three weeks shy of his fifteenth when I had to put him to sleep and could not fulfil my promise to him. This added to my devastation.

I baked a batch of cupcakes anyway, sat on the floor with Suzy and lit a candle. In the flickering candlelight we sang happy birthday and both thought about Max. Well, maybe Suzy was only thinking about the cupcake she was about to devour, but I know she missed having him by her side.

It was a bittersweet birthday celebration filled with deep grief yet swathed in deep love.

Honouring the Love

A couple of days later was the day of his memorial, It was to be a quiet home memorial. My niece and I spent most of the day preparing for our 5pm start. The weather was nice, so I placed a table outside in the garden near where he often lounged in the sun. I moved most things from Lord Max's kitchen table shrine to the outside table: framed photos, framed paw print, a piece of his fur, his collar, lead, a photo collage, his booties and the urn housing his ashes. I decorated it a little more with some bright flowers and soothing candles. A beautiful altar emerged before my eyes in his honour.

I waited in anticipation throughout the day, feeling the grief but eager to proceed.

My family arrived with all sorts of tributes. My nieces brought drawings, cards and poems. I also received as a gift a stone with a lovely inscription for the garden. Each person brought with them stories of Max held deep in their hearts, ready to express and share in our supportive family group. The support and outpouring of love for Max was heart-warming and alleviated the aloneness I had been carrying.

I finally had a moment in time that was all about Max, an opportunity to honour him, discuss him and share his life. He deserved it, and I needed it. It gave me a chance to really be present with my grief.

I was Max's whole life. I would have done anything for him. This was the least I could do, yet I still wanted to do more. How could I repay him for the wonderful laughter, loyalty and love he brought to my life?

All my nieces came to the altar to read their tributes before placing them on the altar. Lastly, it was my turn, and with many heart spills I read my tribute 'My Golden

Light', speaking straight from my soul. My beautiful words to my special Max finally were spoken out loud, allowing me to mourn and release a little more of the grief that was begging to come out.

The rest of the night was all centred on Max. One niece touched my heart by returning many times to the altar to kneel and say another prayer. The others created tonnes of lumi bands for his collar, decorating it like a war hero in coloured plastic, mostly pink.

Suzy was quite sad and mopey. At one point I found her at the altar smelling Max's collar. She then just curled up in front of it, looking up at us as if asking, "Where is Max? I don't understand". She got a lot of extra cuddles that night.

We had dinner as a family and raised our glasses to Max as we shared stories, tears, love and laughter.

Through this memorial experience, the children had a chance to process their grief and understand a bit more about loss and grief, adding to their personal growth. I was also given an opportunity to mourn. We all said our goodbyes that night in our own special way.

But Max is far from gone. His paw prints live on in our conversations, our laughter, our memories, our family and our hearts. His big, goofy, clown smile and silly antics make me smile and can still reduce me to tears. Mostly, my heart is filled with love and laughter.

The candle flickered its beautiful light all night, an apt representation of the eternal light I forever have in my heart. As the stone in the garden reads, 'Gone but never forgotten, always in our hearts', an everlasting, unconditional love is left behind when we lose a pet that continues to fill our hearts.

 Pink Pet Love Note

Happy fifteenth birthday, Max. Beautiful man, forever in my heart...

Tributes

"The bond with a true dog is as lasting as the ties of this earth will ever be."

—Konrad Lorenz

There are endless types of tributes you can arrange or create to honour your pet and your loss. You are only limited by your imagination. Refer back to the *Love and Grief Tools and Strategies* chapter to review some of the ideas we explored such as putting together a photo album, writing a book or a poem, creating a painting, planting a tree or crafting a memory box. All or any are wonderful ways to honour your pet, assisting in the grief and mourning process.

Choose which ones work for you and then put them into place. Stay aware and observe how the grief feels as it begins to shift and move through you. Maybe it comes in waves as it rises and falls through your heart, expressing and withholding at the same time. Give yourself permission to feel everything as you sit with your grief and its energy to get through each day. Practise self-love at each step of this challenging journey.

Some of your tributes may then be delivered at the memorial ceremony depending on how you would like to express them. A eulogy is a form of a tribute used a lot to honour our loved ones. It is commonly delivered at a funeral or a memorial.

Creating a eulogy can be of enormous benefit. You may decide not to have a memorial where it would be read out loud; you may just do it for yourself. But it is still a good exercise as part of your journalling to express your love and feelings on paper. It can be a timeline of their life or simply snippets based on your feelings towards them. Write to your heart's content about your loved pet and what you would like to say to them, or thank them for, or what they brought to your life. It can be written as a poem or prose.

Alternately, you can read your eulogy out at their memorial ceremony or place it on a website as an expression of grief. I did both. On Max's fifteenth birthday, one week after he passed away, I placed my eulogy, 'My Golden Light', as a tribute to Max on the Our Wonderful Pets website (see *Other Helpful Links* for site details) hosted by Katrina Warren. This website provides a space to honour and celebrate your pet. It also provides resources and answers to questions on pet loss. I had read 'My Golden Light' at the memorial and was pleased to have it on the website, honouring Max and my words to him.

I delved deep within as I needed to find a sense of acknowledgement for his life to ensure he was not to be forgotten or diminished by time, life or society. I needed to be sure he mattered, he was important, he had a purpose and he was worthy of only the best I could give him in life and in death. When you lose your pet, you can look for the meaning in their life and in your own. One minute they are here, the next they are not. You look back to photos when they were a puppy then a senior, and now they are gone. How? Why? What is it all about? Things you thought were a big deal during their life suddenly become unimportant. What's the purpose? Why am I here? Why were they here? What does it all mean?

It can certainly throw you into a huge tailspin, running around in circles like a dog chasing its tail. You may try to make sense of your purpose here, of others' purpose and of the meaning of life in general even. It is no different when you lose your people too. The answer does not always appear in a hurry and you will need to practise patience. Sit with the questions that arise and wait for the answers to come. Sometimes they will, maybe they won't. For me, however, sometime later they did.

I began to realise that of course Max had a purpose in life, and in death he taught me so much. I share more on this in *Part 3 The Lessons*. He modelled unconditional love every time he barked, sat, followed me around, begged for treats, was naughty, was a star pupil or laid next to me. Every time I looked intently into his eyes, deep into his soul, I felt the unconditional love transfer from his heart to mine. His soft heartbeats indicated our two souls were connected as one.

It was no different in his death. I followed the paw prints around and around my heart until they answered all the questions that I was desperately seeking answers for. He had relied on me yet protected me. He had needed me yet showed me what it meant to be needed. He dedicated his whole life to me and taught me what it was like to dedicate my life to caring for him. In life he came here to teach me many things, but the most important was about unconditional love. In death the wisdom sunk in even deeper. *The whole point is love!*

I have been lucky to receive this lesson twice on a deep soul and spiritual level. I came to this same realisation after my father's passing, as shared in *Grief, Grace and Gratitude*. This has transformed my life. If you receive this lesson you will find your heart opens to love again. You can acknowledge the grief internally and be open to it rather than closing down. You begin to believe you can cope with anything, so you continue to allow love in and feel the whole rainbow of emotions – good and not so good. This brings a beautiful aliveness and a profound love to your life. Because *the whole point is love!*

Somehow, placing my tribute onto Our Wonderful Pets website helped to appease the questions and feelings I was having. It made the whole experience a little more real, allowing some acceptance to creep in. Spending time on the site, I found myself surrounded by likeminded people and their similarly real and raw loss.

I had a place to be and to learn, to heal and to grieve, to grow and to mourn. This is an example of the type of external support we can seek in our grief journey as mentioned in *Love and Grief Tools and Strategies*. I began to realise that none of us are really alone. You just need to know where to find the people at that time who can help you journey through your loss, and be open to receive this help. Remember to pick these people wisely, especially in the case of pet loss.

Pink Pet Love Note

Goodbye for now, Max. Forever shine your golden light...

Resting Place

"Love is a four-legged word."

—Unknown

The time may come for you to consider your pet's resting place. A resting place gives you a place to go and sit with your pet to focus on the love and the memories. Again, there are a myriad of ways to approach this. Sometimes a resting spot is not where your pet is physically laid to rest. It can be a symbolic place in the garden that you use as your spot to connect with them. You may plant a special tree or lay a special stone. A safe and sacred

Honouring the Love

spot. You will, at some point, think about packing some of your pet's things away. There is never a time limit and you should never be pressured to do this. However, I believe if you pay attention, your inner world will know when the time is right for you. If you are second-guessing yourself, maybe it's not yet that time. Listen intently and go at your own pace.

After Max's memorial, I finally allowed myself to gather the things from Lord Max's shrine and place them in a specially picked cardboard box: cards, letters, poems, collar, boots and everything else that was his except his lead and the urn. My kitchen table became empty, which seemed a little strange for a few days. Fearing it would increase my grief, I checked within and found that my heart remained full.

The time had felt right. If I had tried to do this before I was ready, I would have felt I was boxing him up. After the memorial things had shifted, and I knew I didn't need to cling so much to the material things to recall the love. The love was sitting deep in my heart.

I hung his lead in the laundry where it still hangs many years later, and his urn moves around the house depending on how I feel. Sometimes he sits on the window ledge and other times beside my bed. Next, I decided to create a special Max place in the garden where I could visit. This space began with the stone that my sister gave me at the memorial. I added a few more stones that I collected from his favourite park, a handmade rusty metal heart that was specially made for him, a special tumbled river stone pet memorial and a couple of cute succulent plants.

It took a couple of years to fully create Max's place in the garden. Each step was timely, soothing and allowed his space to grow exactly as it has evolved to be – perfect.

I often get out Max's box and look at his things. I move his urn to a new place or sit near his space in the garden and just spend time remembering. As I close my eyes, I can almost feel him beside me, placing his paw on my lap and demanding another pat just as he had done lovingly so many times.

> ### 🐾 Pink Pet Love Note 🐾
>
> I sit with you, Max, and remember you. The memories I hold are as vivid as the clear blue sky...

Rituals

"Dogs have given us their absolute all. We are the centre of their universe. We are the focus of their love and faith and trust. They serve us in return for scraps. It is without a doubt the best deal man has ever made."

—Roger Caras

Grief assimilates within and comes and goes in waves. You will need to find your strength as you ride the waves and feel whatever feelings your heart sends you on any particular day. It's all temporary, and emotions will move through you like an energy that has been waiting, wanting to be expressed. Ride the waves as they occur and you will feel the grief process more fully, which allows the love to surface and become more available. Anniversaries, such as your pet's birthday, the date they first joined your family, the date of their death, Christmas and other special dates and milestones all present opportunities to process and heal your grief some more.

These are a time to cry, mourn, laugh, honour and celebrate our pet's lives. The early ones can be the most difficult. Anniversaries

Honouring the Love

can bring strong waves of emotion and new heights of grief to process and heal. However, they can help your grief and any emotions you may be repressing. Allowing mourning to occur can clear a little more of your grief outwardly. Anniversaries are loving and create a sense of life as you celebrate their lives once again.

I don't believe grief ever really goes away; you just learn to live with it. It becomes a part of who we are – a beautiful internal scar, as individual as each of us, with the edges sutured together by the love held by two souls. Grief is a bizarre dichotomy. It's the grief and the love in the same heart filling and creating the same scar, both battling for space as we walk our journey of loss. Some days we feel more grief, some days more love. Some days we may feel absolutely nothing.

The internal scar will heal given time and energy. But it will not heal with time alone. It also needs an injection of our added energy to do the grief work. It may break open at times and make us feel like we are moving backwards or circling around. But with the ability and desire to keep moving forward combined with the awareness of our grief and willingness to give energy to our healing, we will arrive at a point where we feel healed, open and loving once again.

Unfortunately, not everyone may reach this stage, or they may flounder at different stages for longer. If so, go back inside to your heart and just notice one paw print at a time. Follow their lead and then pick up on the next. These paw prints are the secret keys to the road home to yourself and have been left by your pet in the form of unconditional love.

You may find that by default you do something on the anniversary that turns into a ritual. Or you may plan what you would like to do. Maybe you sit with them in their resting place, light a candle, sit in meditation or bake cupcakes as I do. As I mentioned earlier, I made cupcakes for Max's fifteenth birthday despite him not being here to eat one. This has turned into a ritual for us, and now each year on Max's birthday I bake cupcakes. (Keep in mind that I don't ever bake anything else.)

With heartfelt precision and my amateur baking skills, I complete a batch of about twenty-four vegan cupcakes. While they are still warm, I sit on the floor with a candle in one cupcake with Suzy beside me and we sing happy birthday. We sit and contemplate Max as we eat the cupcakes. I could never forget Max, yet this gives me a deeper sense of honouring him. He is still with me in my heart, just no longer in his physical form. For me, that deserves still to be honoured, especially on his birthday.

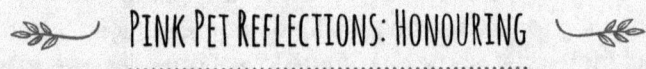

Pink Pet Reflections: Honouring

Use these questions to reflect on how you will honour your pet and the love.

Stop, take a deep breath and reflect. Give yourself permission to go inward, access your Inner Pink Star and the paw prints on your heart. Follow their lead all the way home to the pure, unconditional love of two souls connected as one, holding a love that never dies as you heal your loss, feel the love and appreciate the lessons, knowing that *the whole point is love!*

Honour yourself and your pet and record your feelings in your Pink Pet Grief Journal as you ponder the questions below.

- Would I like to hold a memorial ceremony for my pet? If so, what would I like to include? Who will I invite and where will I hold it?
- Is it time to write a list for all that I need to arrange for the memorial?
- Will the ceremony help me to grieve and mourn?
- Which tributes will honour my pet best?

- 🐾 Will I write a eulogy for my pet?
- 🐾 Do I want to create a resting place? If so, where will it be? What will be part of it?
- 🐾 Are there any rituals I would like to perform for any anniversaries?
- 🐾 What was my pet's purpose? What did they teach me?
- 🐾 What big questions am I currently asking myself about life? Can I sit with patience and stillness to access the answers?
- 🐾 *The whole point is love!* What does this mean to me?
- 🐾 Do I feel the dichotomy of grief and love?
- 🐾 How is the grief assimilating within me? Is my internal scar knitting itself together in a healing fashion?

Well done on completing the questions here. Now might be the time to perform some of the more difficult tasks after losing your pet, using your answers as a guide. Move forward being gentle with yourself and remembering that *the whole point is love!*

If your wish is to write a eulogy, use the following exercise as a guide and my own eulogy for Max, 'My Golden Light', as inspiration (see end of chapter). If not, you can skip to the next chapter.

 Pink Pet Reflections: Eulogy

These questions may guide you as to how you would like to express yourself in your pet's eulogy.

Stop, take a deep breath and reflect. Give yourself permission to go inward, access your Inner Pink Star and the paw prints on your heart. Follow their lead all the way home to the pure, unconditional love of two souls connected as one, holding a love that never dies as you heal your loss, feel the love and appreciate the lessons, knowing that *the whole point is love!*

Honour yourself and your pet and record your feelings in your Pink Pet Grief Journal as you ponder the questions below.

- How did I come to welcome my pet to my family?
- What happened when I brought them home?
- How did I feel, and what did we do on our first day together?
- How did they fit into my life as a puppy/kitten/'baby'?
- Were they easy to train?
- Were they a good teenager?
- Did they grow to an old age? If so, what were they like as a senior?
- What funny things did they do?
- What were their favourite toys and games?
- What were their favourite food and treats?
- Where did they sleep and what were their sleeping habits?

- 🐾 Where were their favourite places that they liked to go to regularly?
- 🐾 Where did they least like to go?
- 🐾 Who were their favourite furry and human friends?
- 🐾 Did they spend much time at the vet? If so, why?
- 🐾 Did I include them on family vacations? If so, where did we go?
- 🐾 What do I remember most? What are my best memories?
- 🐾 What do I miss the most about my pet?
- 🐾 What did they do that made me laugh the most?
- 🐾 Were they the park socialite or more introverted and a homebody?
- 🐾 What strange or funny mannerisms did they have?
- 🐾 What are the biggest learnings and gifts my pet left me?
- 🐾 Do I have any regrets or guilt?
- 🐾 What would I say to them if they were with me now?
- 🐾 What three words would I use to describe them?

Some sentence starters may also help access what is in your heart:

1. I thank you for…
2. I learnt from you…
3. You made me feel…
4. I miss it when…
5. I would love to tell you that…
6. In your honour I will…
7. My favourite thing to say to you was…

8. My favourite thing to do with you was…

9. My favourite nickname for you was…

10. You always made me laugh when you…

11. I ask that you forgive me for…

12. I am grateful that…

13. I wish that you…

14. I hope that you…

15. I love you because…

Well done on this difficult exercise. Delving deep can bring up more grief, but it can also highlight the love that resides under the grief, reminding you of the beautiful unconditional love that surrounds your heart. Go slowly and believe you can cope with whatever comes up. Sit with the feelings and allow the emotional energy to pass through you as you write your eulogy.

Pink Pet Love Note

Sitting in the garden watering the succulents, in my mind I can see you drop, wriggle and roll on the grass nearby. I smile as I feel a strong wave of warmth and love surface from within and envelop me. The unconditional love resting in my heart is always there to tap into…

HONOURING THE LOVE

My Golden Light
....

MAX

MY GOLDEN LIGHT

(Maxo, Mano)

17/7/1999 – 22/6/2014

RIP My beautiful baby boy

You came into my life like a golden light, an instant best friend with a heart so full of love to give and a soul full of joy to share with those you loved.

As a puppy you were as cute, cheeky and naughty as can be, keeping us entertained for hours on end with delight.

So beautiful your locks of golden fur, smooth, silky and soft to touch. You were like a gorgeous golden ball of furry love.

Through thick and thin you were always at my side. You never failed to be at the door to greet me with your loving welcome and wagging tail, just wanting to be near the one you loved so dear.

You were always nudging me with your snoz for a pat or a cuddle and ready to give your love to me and the whole family.

Trips to the beach and the park lightened and brought immense joy to parts of my days and made your days complete, just being you and chasing all the other dogs and ensuring we were all safe.

Loss, Love and Lessons

You always had so much fun rolling around on your back on luscious green grass. One of your favourite pastimes.

You were a great big brother to your friend and smoochy confidant Suzy, inseparable from day one when a special bond was built. Every night you let her lick you from ear to ear, creating a wet looking mohawk throughout your hair. Between the two of you, you have stolen big pieces of my heart.

Max, I look back and the years passed too quickly. I know together we lived and loved life to the fullest, but I crave the memories and the love and struggle to let you go.

Life was far too short for such a loving soul; however, the legacy of your teachings will linger with me forever.

The unconditional love you gave has truly awakened my soul, helping me realise what true love really should be.

You approached any situation in your younger years with vigour and enthusiasm, growing into a true gentleman with dignity and grace in your older years. You always approached life with patience and were true to and loved yourself, trusting others and living every moment to its fullest

The day came when life got too hard. Those leggies of yours were old and tired and seizures were appearing out of nowhere, taking your energy and quality of life.

On the last day, Max, I asked for a sign and you gave it to me, still together deciding your fate. You knew the time had come and you gracefully helped me access inside the right decision to make.

The decision I made with peace, but to lose you still consumes me with grief.

In my arms you took your last breath, fulfilling a promise I had made to always be there with you.

Honouring the Love

You have taken a piece of my heart with you, which I hope keeps you at peace. It was a small gift to give to you, one I loved so much. Each passing day I feel hurt, but I also smile and laugh, you filling my heart up with love in remembrance of our lives and the wonderful memories we created together.

I know I will never see you at the gate again, call your name and see you come running, touch and cuddle your golden furs, look deep into your big brown eyes or kiss your cute muzzle. But in my heart I know you are with me looking down from above, keeping Suzy and me safe till we meet again at Rainbow Bridge and cross over together. Please have fun and enjoy your newfound health and vigour. Don't wait at the gate for me.

I thank you. I miss you and I will love you and remember you forever, more than my heart can express.

Goodbye for now, Max. Forever shine your golden light.

Your mum, Lara, and your best friend, Suzy.

Xxxxx

Loving a New Pet

"The risk of love is loss and the price of loss is grief. But the pain of grief is only a shadow when compared with the pain of never risking love."

—Hilary Stanton Zunin

When will you know you are ready to love a new fur child and welcome them to your family? I believe you just do. When we push it too hard or too early it feels awkward, difficult or even wrong. When we find the right moment, we proceed without too much effort. There is no resistance.

It is paramount to trust yourself and believe you will know and act accordingly when that moment appears. It's about listening to yourself instead of feeling obligated to follow others' advice. It is never too soon or too late. It is only up to you to decide when you are ready.

Take time and ensure you make a responsible and thought-out decision. Often people make an impulsive decision, maybe believing replacing the pet will eliminate their pain. But if they don't have the time to spend with the new pet, it will most likely become unruly. These are the ones taken to shelters months later. It is very sad when this happens because most pets, especially as puppies, come into a house ready and eager to be good family pets, and it's often our unintentional neglect that sets them up for failure.

If you adopt a new pet, they will need a lot of your time as they adjust to their new surroundings. You need to be patient as they become a good family pet. They have a lot to learn, and all pets want to learn. Do you have the time? Is the whole family ready to make this commitment? A joint family decision is best. You want everyone to be happy about adding to the fur family and not still be deep in mourning and highly emotional lest that upsets a new pet. Also don't forget to consider how any existing pets are going with their grieving and behaviour. Are they ready and able to welcome a new family member?

There is a lot to think about to ensure the smooth transition of a new warm, eager heart to join your family. I believe you will know when the time is right, but just allow a few moments of thought to ensure you can give all that the pet deserves.

Maybe right now you can't imagine ever replacing your pet. Believe me, one pet never replaces another. They are a new loving soul brought to you to add to your family, possibly even sent by your recently departed pet. Our hearts have more than enough love for many pets and people in our lives. It's just a matter of opening up our broken heart to shower that love on the new soul waiting patiently to be welcomed to your world.

Many fear they will not overcome the present hurts and that the same thing will happen again and they won't be able to cope. So they decide against getting another pet to prevent the hurt. Their heart may remain a little closed, or at least not be able to be opened fully. I totally get this. Grief hurts!

However, if you walk through your grief pain, facing each day and emotion as it arises, you will find the love on the other side. Yes, it will hurt if it happens again, but each experience of grief helps to teach us that we can cope. Each time we approach grief with an openness to feel and move forward we open our hearts a little more to love, creating space for another soul and more love to enter.

To me, all the grief was well worth the love and happiness Max brought me. So after I walked through the pain, 18 months since Max's passing, I started to feel a shift in the form of a paw print on my heart that was leading me to a new family member. At first it was just a little nudge; I started contemplating getting a little golden retriever puppy. After speaking to some breeders and putting my name down on some lists, something didn't feel quite right. I had only ever imagined getting another puppy, so I was perplexed as to why it felt wrong.

One night I sat in meditation and asked myself the question, "Is the time right to get a puppy?" and an astounding NO came all over me. I realised that with all I had on my plate at that time in life, I was far too busy and stressed to bring a puppy into my world and provide what it needed. My dad had been very unwell with a terminal illness and our family were spending time looking after him. I was a little distraught and did not want to add to my stress levels. Plus I didn't have time to train a puppy and give it all it deserved to have the best start in life.

So, I started playing around on the Pet Rescue website looking at adult pets needing a home. I had never rescued an animal, so it was a little leftfield for me. But it felt like a possibility. Pet Rescue is a little like a dating website. You can view all the profiles and swipe right for yes or left for no. But I wanted to adopt them all! They each had unique stories, and all looked longingly into the lens, pleading you to take them and give them a family and a warm bed of their own. Then late one night one furry soul caught my eye. She was a black Labrador, a senior at eleven years old, and her name was Chelsea. She was beautiful. It was love at first sight. Chelsea was fully trained so I would just need to settle her in.

Within minutes I sent an email to the address they provided and explained my story and how I wanted to meet this beautiful dog. The very next day, she paraded down my driveway with her lead and teddy bear in tow, waiting eagerly for an introduction.

Chelsea was lucky in that she's had a normal doggy life until she was given up due to relocation reasons. She then spent only one week in foster care and fortunately escaped any time on the concrete floor of the pound. She wagged her tail on her entrance and proceeded to make herself at home, as Labradors do. She was easily persuaded by any form of food. She had me at woof!

She stayed for a two-week trial, but within 24 hours I knew Chelsea was my new fur baby. I consulted with Suzy who agreed with a big woof. Chelsea battered her beautiful brown eyes at me as a big thank you. There was not one moment of doubt, worry or justification on my part. I just opened my heart and she fell softly into it. I just knew! She moved in.

My plan was always to get another golden retriever puppy. However, reality turned out to be something so different yet utterly wonderful. You never know what is around the corner, but if you can keep your heart open, life continues to surprise you with beautiful gifts.

Maybe Max was sending a ray of golden light in the form of Chelsea. This senior nanna black Labrador makes me laugh every day. Losing Max broke my heart into a million pieces, but my path of grief led me to find I had more than enough love to shower over a new furry soul. Chelsea returns it tenfold. I couldn't be any happier or luckier.

I haven't forgotten Max. As I mentioned in *Resting place*, I see reflections of him everywhere in my home: his urn, his lead in the laundry, his name disc in my purse and pictures of him everywhere. Then there is the whole wall mural in the doggy feeding area. Mostly Max lays spread throughout my heart. His paw prints continue to guide me forward, enveloped by his love and the lessons he gifted me during his life and in his passing.

Do you feel like you have the potential to extend your open heart that is now full of love to loving another furry child? Maybe the time is right; maybe you are not quite there yet. Always go at your own pace with what feels right to you. The following Pink Pet Reflection may assist you in this.

Pink Pet Reflections: Is this the time?

Stop, take a deep breath and reflect. Give yourself permission to go inward, access your Inner Pink Star and the paw prints on your heart. Follow their lead all the way home to the pure, unconditional love of two souls connected as one, holding a love that never dies as you heal your loss, feel the love and appreciate the lessons, knowing that *the whole point is love!*

Honour yourself and your pet and record your feelings in your Pink Pet Grief Journal as you ponder the questions below.

- 🐾 How do I feel about getting another pet?
- 🐾 Are my family and other pets ready to receive an addition to our family?
- 🐾 Have I got the time to devote to welcoming and training my new pet?
- 🐾 Is the time right for me?
- 🐾 Do I trust my inner ability to know when it's right?

Let's move forward now with the love that you hold to heal your loss a little more. It's time to reflect on the beautiful lessons your furry friends teach you in their passing about living a deeply rich and purposeful life.

Love Contemplations

- 🐾 The grief journey is one of both grief and deep love. I hope you now understand that without grief there is no love and that you are uncovering the love that has been shrouded by the grief.

- 🐾 The human-animal bond is so beautifully raw, with your furry friend gifting and modelling to you every day pure unconditional love. No wonder pet loss cuts so deep.

- 🐾 The love and grief models and their stages have hopefully helped you to process your grief. Your love-grief toolbox is now full of healing ideas, which you are putting into place.

- 🐾 There are many ways to honour your pet such as a memorial, a tribute or a eulogy.

- 🐾 Despite being launched into the rainbow of emotions through your grief, you can learn how to unlock the love that lies within at the other end of the grief and loss. It's feeling this love that leads you forward with an open heart. Be gentle with yourself. It does take time.

Feel the love!

Pink Pet Love Note

The time was finally right to welcome another furry soul into my life. Thank you, Max, for helping my heart to heal and burst open with love to enable the most loving welcome to Princess Chelsea...

PART 3

The Lessons

Learnings from a Dog's Life: Max's Manifesto

"Dogs do speak, but only to those who know how to listen."

—Orhan Pamuk

The final stage of the grief path is where we begin to look at the countless learnings from our pet's life. It's a show of wisdom to look back and reflect on our life or our grief and notice how far we have come, and what it has gifted us. So, let's do that now.

You have travelled through the raw grief, reading about Max's story and contemplating your own. Then you learnt about the human-animal bond, why pet grief in our society is so difficult and that allowing your grief to have a voice is imperative to your healing and finding the love that awaits you.

You then looked at two grief models and the stages that grief takes you through. From there you explored many grief tools and strategies to help you process this grief. Maybe now you, and perhaps your children, have created tributes, written a eulogy and had a memorial. Maybe you even have a new furry family member. If so, congratulations and welcome!

So, now it's time to reflect some more on what your pet has taught you.

Our pets model to us many positive traits in their simple lives. If we integrate these into our own life, we can experience life as a little less complicated and a little more joyful. Maybe a lot! I believe we can become better humans and strive to live out our life purpose. One of the mysteries – and miracles – of life is that in living their purpose, our dogs help us live ours, if we are intuitive and reflective.

Max's life was a great adventure for him, and he learnt many things in his short life with me. Likewise, he fulfilled his purpose and taught me many things, which I will carry with me through the rest of my life. Dogs are shining stars that light up our lives so brightly and pull us out of our stress and confusion. They allow us to experience a little happiness. Just the pure action of nudging us with their wet noses to find a warm place in our lap can take us out of our worries and place us gently into the present moment.

Life for most of us has become chaotic and busy. Many of us live in fear, denial, stress, confusion, anxiety and depression. We are 'yes' people, strive for perfection, become achievement junkies, overanalyse and worry about everything. All this becomes the new normal, yet it is eons from where we are supposed to reside. Looking at your pet and the way it lives gifts you the opportunity to take stock and maybe take a different route in life.

Grief shakes you up and takes you on a long journey through the centre of your soul. When you come to the latter part of it and reflect deeply and assimilate the lessons your pets model to you, you are often transformed. This can take a lot of different paths. You may leave your corporate existence and take up yoga. You may move from a busy city to a quiet seaside town. You perhaps seek and uncover your purpose and see how you can incorporate that into your life. Maybe your life pretty much stays the same, but the paw prints on your heart highlight a host of beautiful lessons deep within that see you changing a little at your heart space.

Learnings from a Dog's Life: Max's Manifesto

Life is filled with positive and negative experiences that are just part of being human. However, it is possible to live a life with less drama and chaos and instead fill it with love and joy. It is your decision to take ownership of your life, accept responsibility and design the life you want. Dogs make it simple. They smell the roses, and more, underneath their friend's tails. They are a joy to watch and to learn from, and in doing so, we can modify our lives for the better. We just need to become more aware of this instead of wandering around in a dreamlike state as we go about our daily realities.

Grief changes you and opens you up to your vulnerabilities. It also gifts you the lessons and opportunity to do things differently, for the better. To grow and to emerge healed, open and full of unconditional love. It hands you a beautiful gift from your late pet to be more like them, to stop for a minute and see if your life is how you expected it to be. If not, it allows you to make changes.

Sometimes the lessons take a while to surface when immersed in your grief. But if you keep your eyes open and create self-awareness, you will be presented with subtle clues or messages from within that create the small shifts inside.

It is in our most difficult moments that we grow the most. But we need to be open to that growth, and from it we change. We know better, we do better, we feel better and life opens like a beautiful flower in springtime. This part of our grief is like giving us permission to be reborn, reassessing how we live, act, feel, think and behave. Be with ourselves, change, blossom and grow.

I've brought together in this part of the book the key lessons I've learnt from having Max in my life and in his passing. No doubt you will relate to them too. Taking on board these lessons can help you move out of any remaining negative states and to be kinder and more self-loving towards yourself. You can be the person your pet would like you to be: the person they are role modelling to you.

The lessons guide you to live a balanced, happy and healthy life – the simple life principles that every dog naturally lives by. In recognising these, you may be able to treasure even more the gifts of your furry friend and move more easily from loss and grief through the lessons to unconditional love.

I believe this is why we have pets! To teach us how to be better humans.

I am sure that Max, like me, wishes for you to find the beauty and magnificence in the lessons that follow.

Welcome to what I call *Max's Manifesto*!

Unconditional love

🐾 *Max's Manifesto says: Give and receive unconditional love – the most beautiful kind of love where no limitations or conditions are placed and you can be your beautiful self.*

Unconditional love is love without conditions. It is where love is given freely to our loved ones no matter what and with no limitations. It is being solely concerned with the happiness of another and what we can do to enable that happiness without expecting anything in return. Our pets, while living and in their passing, also model to us the gift and lessons of unconditional love, which, like grief, transform us and our lives.

If you had a dog, picture them a moment and think about how they always showered you with love no matter what. Even if you fed them late, missed your daily walk, chastised them for bringing muddy paws inside or omitted giving them a treat despite their begging, they still loved you boundlessly and fully. Dogs still feel pain and suffering, but they have the ability to forgive, forget and to bounce back, loving us unconditionally providing we give them the right environment and love.

LEARNINGS FROM A DOG'S LIFE: MAX'S MANIFESTO

In this world where we are surrounded by conditional love – a love that with limitations expects something in return and can destroy relationships at its worst – we have a lot to learn to mimic our dog's wise behaviours and be able to love the way they do. They are the epitome of unconditional love. After your dog's passing, that love still resides in your memories and heart. This allows you in turn to give and receive the same sort of love with other humans and other furry, feathery and scaly friends.

Dogs let us be who we are. They drop any expectations and don't try to change us, unless of course we hurt them. Some may then let us know it is not acceptable. But let's focus here on the lesson. Like our pets, we need to practise letting people be who they are, without trying to change someone for our own benefit. This forces us to look at ourselves and find our own strength within to love ourselves enough to permit others not to have to fill the gaps and the voids we hold deep inside.

This process can be particularly challenging. Allowing this to happen may draw to the surface all our innocence, insecurities and vulnerabilities. It compels us to make changes inside, release the ego and drop the masks we wear to survive daily. To live in love and not fear, finding the love in all situations and then willingly showering this love out to others, is not an easy task. But it is one we can walk towards when we better understand the theory of it.

Our dogs spent all their days living in this way. They lived with an open heart full of devotion for their owner, modelling unconditional love at every butt wiggle. They didn't live in fear but in the love, always willing to open up, cuddle, nudge, paw and show their affection. Despite how many times we may push our pet's paw or nose away when we are busy, they continue to love us unconditionally with a full heart. They are selfless.

We can learn a lot more about loving relationships from our furry friends. They run to greet us at the door

Live with an open heart.

each time we arrive home, no matter how late we are. Ecstatic to have us home, with a huge wag of the tail and a butt wiggle, our excitable pet runs up the hallway, grabbing a toy for us or howling a cry of delight – their way to show us their love.

There is no nagging or complaining that we are ten minutes late or dumping the negative parts of their day on us, like when the postman disrupted their sleep or that we didn't call them during the day. They are just grateful and happy to have us back. This is why some of us are more excited sometimes to see our dogs after a long day than our children or partners because the dogs expect nothing. It is a simple and beautiful way of being without all the pressure.

Dogs tell us in doggy language how they feel about us all the time. All we need to do is look into their eyes, deep into their soul, and we can see it reflected back to us. They don't keep their feelings bottled up, hoping we can read their mind. They don't fear rejection. They open up and give and receive love fully and purely. They make deep connections right down to the soul and beyond.

Dogs show acceptance always that we are doing the best we can with what we know. They don't question but give us the benefit of the doubt. What a great philosophy for us humans to adopt with our fellow friends and loved ones.

Dogs are a pillar of support, quietly sitting with us and listening to our woes. They never try to fill the silences. They simply listen, head in lap, soothing us with that magical elixir. They allow us to talk, cry, vent and finally come to our own quiet acceptance of our situation. They give us space to find within ourselves the solution to our problems. They help our woes melt away gracefully and naturally. Our pets don't disappear to protect their own feelings from arising that they haven't dealt with yet. They don't tell us to stop crying when in fact we need to clear the teary energy from our body.

Learnings from a Dog's Life: Max's Manifesto

We humans, on the other hand, often want to help so much that we don't even let another person finish talking before offering advice. We mean well yet we are not standing in their shoes. We have an opportunity here to be observant to what someone needs.

The best advice to generally give someone is no advice. Allow them to come to their own solution by active listening. We are often so bombarded with many people offering us advice for our problems, we only get more overwhelmed, not knowing which way to go. This may be especially true when we are experiencing grief emotions and people try to talk us out of them! Sitting with ourselves and just talking out loud generally can lead us to the solution for ourselves without any noisy interference from others. Don't forget meditation.

Dogs are particularly good at this because obviously they can't talk. Maybe this is how it was designed so they could be great listeners and teach us this. They invest in their relationships, often hot on your heels wherever you go, even the bathroom. They are not immersed in their devices or distracted with the latest craze or chore. They are there for us always.

Be like them. Be with the ones you love. Let your loved ones be the ones who bring the best out in you. Unconditionally love your loved ones. Find your strength and openness to give unconditional love all the time even if it is not always given in return. One small act on your behalf or a change in your behaviour can in turn change someone else's. You can shift the behaviour of others just by shifting yours.

Be immaculate with your words when you talk about others, remove yourself from gossiping and ensure you don't start the gossip trail. People are doing the best they can in this tricky world. Try and find a more productive habit or purpose for your conversations than raining on others' lives and bringing them down.

Loss, Love and Lessons

We all suffer our own distress and difficulties and need as many people as possible in our corner when we seek support. The more we love ourselves and learn about unconditional love the more we can love others and give others what they need instead of tearing them down, unintentionally or not.

Don't let others mistake your kindness and love for weakness though. You still deserve respect. If you are being disrespected and not treated how you deserve, it is also loving to ask for what you want and need. If this is not possible, you can quietly slip away from the relationship, but ensure you are sending them love as you leave. This is the key.

Do you know why so many of us are unhappy and stressed? It is because our expectations of others or situations don't meet our reality. There is a massive gap. This massive gap is the source of the suffering. Sometimes we must have expectations, but if we are able to softly release our expectations of others and allow them to be themselves, often we can learn to accept reality for what it is.

Simply understand that sometimes life is good and sometimes bad. Life is always just what it is and if we can learn to go with the flow a little more and accept whatever comes our way, it becomes a little easier to navigate.

Dropping some of our resistance and expectations of life, and of our grief, makes life a much more comfortable place to reside. Every moment is extraordinary and is just a different experience for us to traverse, leaving us more lessons and gifts to learn.

LEARNINGS FROM A DOG'S LIFE: MAX'S MANIFESTO

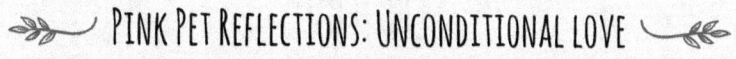 PINK PET REFLECTIONS: UNCONDITIONAL LOVE

Stop, take a deep breath and reflect. Give yourself permission to go inward, access your Inner Pink Star and the paw prints on your heart. Follow their lead all the way home to the pure, unconditional love of two souls connected as one, holding a love that never dies as you heal your loss, feel the love and appreciate the lessons, knowing that *the whole point is love!*

Let's reflect on each lesson as we progress through Part 3 and see how it relates to you. Are you changing or transforming through your grief and your lessons as you work towards healing? Honour yourself and your pet and record your feelings in your Pink Pet Grief Journal as you ponder the questions below.

- 🐾 What have I learnt about unconditional love?
- 🐾 What have I learnt about unconditional love from my pet?
- 🐾 Can I integrate this unconditional love into my being and my life?
- 🐾 Am I open to receiving unconditional love?
- 🐾 Am I open to giving unconditional love to others?

Contemplate and integrate this lesson while you move forward in your grief and your healing. Love life fully. Be open to the world and the experiences that present themselves, including the grief journey, and give a woof no matter what comes along. Be like Max. Run to the door to meet your loved ones and shower them with unconditional love every time.

Self-love

🐾 *Max's Manifesto says: Be self-loving and live in the peaceful place where you continually grow physically, mentally, emotionally and spiritually. Where you know, honour and accept all parts of yourself.*

Self-love is important because we can only love others as much as we can love ourselves. We can only receive love as much as we can love ourselves. So if you cannot love yourself, you cannot genuinely love another.

Dogs can give and receive an endless supply of unconditional love, which is initiated by their own self-love. To fully receive that love from them, you must accept it. To accept it is to say you are worthy to accept it and are worthy of love. That is self-love. So you could say that self-love is the ultimate key to learn and love in life. You now know *the whole point is love!* And I say it begins with self-love. What a wonderful lesson from your pet!

Self-love is *not* narcissism where there is a lack of empathy for others and a strong need for admiration alongside arrogance and self-centredness. In this space we think we are better than others, instead of feeling like equals. Self-love instead comes from a beautiful inner space that feels true and authentic, warm and furry.

I see self-love as a calm and peaceful state that helps us to grow in our physical, mental, emotional and spiritual being. When we reside here, through loving actions to self, we know ourselves well and accept who we are with all our strengths and areas for improvement. We take responsibility for our life and are the author of our life and master of our own destiny.

We know ourselves intimately and our joy comes from what happens on the inside rather than the external. This is often a long and tumultuous journey, but it is well worth the rewards.

LEARNINGS FROM A DOG'S LIFE: MAX'S MANIFESTO

Sadly, we are not always brought up in a society that supports us in loving ourselves. Many of us have self-esteem issues. We are taught to stay quiet and not be ourselves, to not outshine others and instead please others at all costs. All this stresses us while we quietly suffer. Some of us are also taught that unconditional love means loving others at our complete expense. So, it can become a very difficult task later in life when we realise that we are not treating ourselves in the loving way that we are worthy of, and our heart is in anguish.

When we face grief, we can become even less self-loving as we try to negotiate the grief terrain and the rainbow of emotions. Sometimes we struggle just to survive. It's overwhelming. Without self-love, our self-esteem can plummet further and we may seek undesirable ways to fill our emptiness, push our feelings down and avoid our deep grief. Yet we need to feel all these feelings to move through our grief and unearth the love that lies below.

With self-love, however, your life begins to sparkle. It begins to take on a lightness that sees you leaping out of bed in the mornings, ready to face another day knowing you are a good person with a strong purpose in our world. You feel able to sit with yourself and feel your feelings. You slowly treat yourself with respect while navigating the rough and windy road of grief in search of healing.

Self-love has many faces. Mostly it is about appreciating, accepting, respecting, honouring and valuing yourself. It grows from actions that support this. It is about treating your physical, emotional, mental and spiritual self with extreme care and love.

Below are some examples of actions of self-love you can take. How about developing your own list of self-loving actions? Set some small goals and start to action them.

- 🐾 make decisions that are best for you
- 🐾 commit to taking the entire grief journey
- 🐾 rebuild yourself through the grief process
- 🐾 believe in yourself and trust your ability to heal

Loss, Love and Lessons

- know what you think, feel and want
- act on what you want
- remain calm and centred as you move forward
- forgive others to free yourself from their binds
- remove unnecessary drama from your life
- face and feel your emotions and deal with them
- stop and rest when you need to
- eat, drink, exercise and sleep as needed
- find a balance in life
- protect yourself from negative, unhelpful comments
- remove yourself from negative or toxic situations
- set boundaries with others and say no
- protect yourself from unsupportive people
- give your heart only to loving, kind and nurturing people
- accept your mistakes and forgive yourself
- release unrealistic expectations
- drop the achievement junkie attitude
- stop the comparison game
- do what makes you happy
- celebrate your wins
- be aware of what is happening internally
- truly understand your desires and needs
- allow yourself to have lots of fun and laughter
- surround yourself with your likeminded tribe
- live in and enjoy the present moment
- live with intention, passion and purpose
- express your heart
- find your creativity and share it with the world
- nourish and nurture your body, mind and heart
- love all of you
- sit quietly with yourself, calmly and peacefully
- be proud of who you are, with grace and dignity

Learnings from a Dog's Life: Max's Manifesto

- 🐾 commit to changing and growing where needed
- 🐾 say "I love me".

Dogs are excellent at living with self-love, and you can be too with a little education and time spent evaluating where you are at and what small changes in life you can make.

You generally have two choices in your grief:

- 🐾 You can run and hide from the grief and suppress and repress the emotions, which will generally build up and explode sometime later, OR
- 🐾 You can stop and face your grief, walk to the centre of it and deal with it like a self-loving adult would.

I love me.

Your grief will often force you to stop and look for a different way of living. This may include seeking some self-awareness. When you have this awareness and begin to look for new ways to do things and look after yourself, you have begun the self-love journey. Life begins to change in a positive way.

~ Pink Pet Reflections: Self-love ~

Stop, take a deep breath and reflect. Give yourself permission to go inward, access your Inner Pink and the paw prints on your heart. Follow their lead all the way home to the pure, unconditional love of two souls connected as one, holding a love that never dies as you heal your loss, feel the love and appreciate the lessons, knowing that *the whole point is love!*

Honour yourself and your pet and record your feelings in your Pink Pet Grief Journal as you ponder the questions below.

- 🐾 What have I learnt about self-love?
- 🐾 What have I learnt from my pet about self-love?
- 🐾 Can I be more self-loving?
- 🐾 What strategies can I adopt to be more self-loving?
- 🐾 What would be different in my life if I could be more self-loving?

Contemplate and integrate this lesson while you move forward in your grief and your healing. Grief and loss can completely change you, and you get to decide if that is for the better or the worse. Like Max, your late doggy would want you to pick up every lesson just like when you took them for a walk and they sniffed a thousand smells, taking them all in. Similarly, you can take in every sense, feeling and emotion and gather them all together inside with a loving self-awareness that helps you to move forward without your furry loved one. In time, you will find your own big clown smile in their honour.

Health

- 🐾 *Max's Manifesto says: Live a healthy life physically, mentally, emotionally and spiritually. Make sure you eat a varied healthy diet, exercise routinely, and sleep well to heal and restore your body. In general, consider all aspects of a healthy life that lead to your own homeostasis, that is, balance.*

LEARNINGS FROM A DOG'S LIFE: MAX'S MANIFESTO

I am presuming you are a good owner and take your furry friends in yearly or bi-annually for their vaccinations, flea, heartworm and worming treatment, feed them good food, provide a warm safe bed, exercise them regularly and take care of all their other health needs. You take responsibility for their health, and it is a big responsibility. Just like you they have needs and wants. You notice when they seem out of sorts, aren't eating or pooping properly or are lethargic. Then it's off to the vets. Their good health is vital for them to live and for you to have your furry companions with you. So what about your health?

Without your health you have nothing and can lose everything! Do you agree?

If losing our pets due to their health doesn't teach us this, what will? Well, when we don't have our health, we realise even more how important our health is. For years we may take our physical vessel for granted. Our body carries us around and we commonly don't think too much about it, especially when we are younger. Many of us are disconnected from our physical body.

As we age, we become more stressed, our lives become busier, our unhealthy diets take their toll and initiate inflammation and our digestion may start to falter. Bang, suddenly niggles start. If we continue to live in denial and don't listen to the body's gentle messages, these little niggles may turn into more serious complaints. If we continue to ignore the body, it may begin screaming at us. Then we have a disease that may take years to cure, if at all.

Some of us use this illness as a wakeup call. If we are lucky at this stage and escape more serious issues, we may wish we had respected our body earlier. We promise now, at all costs, to honour it and change our lifestyle as we move forward.

You do all you can for your fur children to be with you for as long as possible. So, how about applying a little of this thinking to your own life? Visit the doctor yearly for a check-up and have your blood tests done. Scan your body regularly for any concerns and get on top of any issue quickly. It's wise to live in the preventative stage of disease rather than the sick-and-fix-it stage. Pay attention!

Have you looked at your diet lately? Are you eating a nourishing wholefood diet and removing things that aren't healthy for you? If not, what one small thing could you do to make a difference?

Generally, we all know where we could improve in this respect. It's just a matter of doing it. When we find it difficult, it's usually related to our emotional health. Food and alcohol are an effective guise for emotional issues and to deal with stress. We all know how yummy Tim Tams or a packet of chips are, or how tempting a table full of delicious food is in social and family situations. I follow the 80/20 rule, that is, 80 percent of the time try to be good and for the other 20 percent you can have a little treat. If you flip this theory, along comes inflammation and right on its heels comes disease.

Dogs do know a few things about their health though. For a start, they definitely know how to sleep. For them, the most natural and luxurious thing to do is to nap all day while we go out and earn the big bucks to buy the cute dog bed they laze in. On a nice sunny day, they will go outside and find the sunniest napping spot where they can soak up giant rays of vitamin D to support their bodies.

When they are tired, they lay their head to nap. They instinctively know that sleep is important to rest and heal the body. They sleep so they can prepare their body for their next adventure: getting to know their surroundings, community, the next-door-neighbour's dog or just the local tree around the corner that houses enchanting smells. They love to step out of their comfort zones and discover new things and places.

Getting enough quality sleep helps to protect your mental, physical and emotional health and general quality of life. It is equally good for the brain to prepare for the upcoming day and all its challenges. Starting the day with movement, even a few stretches, allows your

LEARNINGS FROM A DOG'S LIFE: MAX'S MANIFESTO

body to wake up gently, enables your joints to be lubricated and keeps the spine healthy. Even five to ten minutes at the start of your day will ensure a better morning and a happier body. When our dogs awaken, they will do a downward dog, stretch it out and get on with the next job on their daily list, which is normally eating or pooping.

Our dogs also relish their daily outing, hoping for a bigger walk to the doggy park. There they shake off any tension and negativity while their paws walk 'barefoot' in the soil. It's called earthing or grounding. Earthing is being in contact with the earth and allowing the subtle natural energy to flow up through our feet. Its benefits include improved circulation, better sleep, equalising blood pressure, stress reduction, faster recovery from muscular strain, improved energy, and reduced pain and inflammation. Connecting to the earth is like recharging your energy and rebalancing your body's system. Dogs have surely known this from the beginning, else they would all be wearing little dog booties. It's easy to do. You just need a park and bare feet, like when you were a kid. Try it.

Being around other people in the fresh air while moving your body is the best thing for the health of your mind, body and heart. Dogs know this, and they enjoy socialising with all their friends and sniffing a lot of behinds. Everyone likes a well-socialised dog, and as humans we also need to be around other people. It's smart and healthy to have support from likeminded people, especially during our grief.

Dogs always seem to maintain a positive attitude and start the day on the right paw. They feel their emotions when they rise and then shake them off once the energy has passed. They hope for the best and believe always that a big juicy marrow bone is in each shopping bag that enters the house. Likewise, being positive and full of hope helps your physical health and keeps you stronger and protects you from disease. As the body, mind and heart are all linked, it's important to focus on all the areas in unison.

One more life-improving thing you can learn from your wise furry friends is simply how to breathe. Have you ever sat for a moment and watched your dog breathe? They take a deep breath, drinking in the air and filling the lower abdomen through to their rib cage all the way up to their collar bones. They completely fill their lung cavity, pause at the top of the inhale and gently exhale, and begin the cycle again. It's like a gentle and slow wave of air moving and rippling through the body.

You will remember in *Love and Grief Tools and Strategies* that I shared the benefits of mindfulness, meditation and your breath, all elements of yoga. If you stop and pay attention to your breath, note how often you shallow breathe from your upper chest only. This type of breathing initiates anxiety. Breathing correctly from deep in your abdomen can instantly take you out of your anxiety, change your state and bring your body into a state of calm, reducing stress.

Give it a try now and see how your system responds. Putting your hands on your lower rib cage helps. You will generally be rewarded with a feeling of peace and calmness. As the thoughts appear, allow them to rise and let them go, bring your mind back to the breath and just breathe. (If you need more prompts, go to the long meditation in the *Appendix*.)

Breathe

Deep abdominal breath works with your parasympathetic nervous system and puts the body into rest and digest function, helping it to maintain balance and heal as needed. Perhaps you run more on your sympathetic nervous system in times of stress, following the fight-or-flight response.

In this state your body can shut down some of your systems, like your digestion, so you can fight the sabre tooth tiger in the room, which today is the mountain of paperwork and chores waiting to be done. When your system stays in the fight-or-flight system with no respite, you can quickly become more stressed and more ill.

Learnings from a Dog's Life: Max's Manifesto

When I teach yoga, Suzy my golden retriever starts getting a little frisky, not wanting to sit still. Then as I begin the breathing at the start of my practice, she lies down and becomes settled and still. By the end of the class, she is totally zenned out. She loves the meditation and her body energy settles as mine does, and vice versa.

Until I chant 'Om' at the end of class, that is. When I open my eyes I find she has risen and is often a foot away from my face, staring at me. Occasionally, she does a little bark to acknowledge her honouring of self.

Meditate with your pets. It's a lot of fun watching their energy mimic yours.

Overall, it's a matter of finding balance and listening to the body. Just start making some of the changes below, one step at a time. Your mind, body and spirit will thank you.

- get your sleep
- eat well
- stress less
- maintain positivity
- breathe well
- be mindful
- hydrate well
- pee and poop as needed
- don't take life so seriously
- have some fun
- take breaks
- don't overanalyse
- be in the moment
- make the tough decisions
- find solutions
- be proactive
- socialise
- meditate.

Live life with a big clown smile!

It really can be that simple.

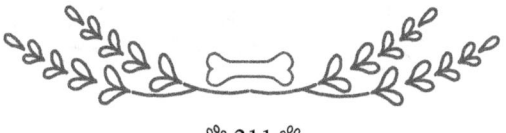

Pink Pet Reflections: Health

Stop, take a deep breath and reflect. Give yourself permission to go inward, access your Inner Pink Star and the paw prints on your heart. Follow their lead all the way home to the pure, unconditional love of two souls connected as one, holding a love that never dies as you heal your loss, feel the love and appreciate the lessons, knowing that *the whole point is love!*

Honour yourself and your pet and record your feelings in your Pink Pet Grief Journal as you ponder the questions below.

- What have I learnt about health?
- What have I learnt from my pet about health?
- Can I work to improve my health?
- What would I need to change to be healthier?
- What would be different in my life if I lived a healthier life?

Contemplate and integrate this lesson while you move forward in your grief and your healing. Don't take your health for granted, listen to your body, mind and heart, and allow them to work together harmoniously as a perfect orchestra of breath. Allow yourself to feel inner joy and contentment. Sound like anyone you know?

"Woof," says Max!

LEARNINGS FROM A DOG'S LIFE: MAX'S MANIFESTO

VALUES

🐾 *Max's Manifesto says: Unearth your values and live by them every day. List your top five and see if you are truly living by them. Where there are some gaps see what you can do differently to begin to transform your life.*

Dogs are a picture of values:

🐾 They hold *hope* for a big chew toy to arrive from your next shopping visit.

🐾 They show *gratefulness* with a big wet lick from just saying hello to them.

🐾 They are *accepting* of our idiosyncrasies.

🐾 They show *patience* while they wait all day for you to arrive home.

🐾 They *forgive* if you snarl at them for doing something naughty.

🐾 They display *loyalty* just by being by your side.

🐾 They show *determination* when they try to bury a huge bone in a tiny hole.

🐾 They demonstrate *happiness* with a big wagging tail.

🐾 They express *kindness* as they sit and bat those big brown eyes at you. They are authentic and quirky in their own way.

🐾 They *please*, living their purpose.

🐾 They display *vitality and playfulness*.

🐾 And most importantly they show unconditional love in each moment.

They live their values.

Essentially, values are who you are! They are the fundamental beliefs that lie deep inside you that motivate and lead you towards certain attitudes and actions. They serve as a guide for your behaviour and are what is important to you and how you live your life.

Strong values help you flow through life even when the toughest problems present themselves to be solved. Not that it may be easy, but you will have the blueprint that will chaperone you going forward. Values help you grow and transform as you journey through your grief.

What values you hold will inform how you act and deal with your grief. They help to create the future that you desire. Without solid values your path can be a little rocky, taking you in different directions or with no clear road ahead. You could find yourself in an uncomfortable rut not knowing what or how to change. Such times during your grief journey present you with an opportunity to check in and make sure the values you hold now are still applicable to the life you wish to evolve into. Grief transforms who you are and, in turn, you may find your values grow and change.

Who am I?

Values help you find your purpose in life or at least help you align a little closer to them once you can know what they are. Maybe you have persistently worked your way up the corporate ladder only to feel miserable, like many of us do. You have the big bucks but alongside that comes the long hours and massive levels of stress. A closer look at your values may reveal that you are more aligned to family and a sense of calmness than that of the busy corporate system. This may highlight to you that it's time for a change. So, listen!

Learnings from a Dog's Life: Max's Manifesto

Even if you cannot make a change just yet, at least you can acknowledge what you need and be honest with yourself. Plan for some changes and how you will bring about the life you desire.

When you live in denial of your values, or out of alignment with them, anxiety and depression may not be far behind. The reason is you are not living authentically – a sure-fire way to create big internal struggles. Values act like a preventative medicine and a buffer to some of these internal issues.

Your values guide your behaviour and how you react to different situations. When you understand and align with your values, your actions will begin to change. Maybe you want to live a calm and quiet life or have in the past reacted hastily to constructive feedback. Setting your values may help you learn to take in feedback, assess it and then respond in a way that fits with your new values.

While you set your values and begin to live by them, you begin to understand yourself better and develop a stronger sense of self. This results in more self-esteem, more confidence and an increase in your overall happiness level. They take you on a road to fulfilment.

Do you have a friend who was the corporate lawyer who left their role to grow mushrooms in a faraway hippie town? They re-evaluated their values, which was possibly preceded by a stressful time of some sort – maybe grief or a different struggle. But, similarly, through their re-evaluation, values evolved and with it a complete change of life – no doubt to a happier and more peaceful existence.

Pink Pet Reflections: Values

There are so many values you could live by. I've shared above what dogs do to express their values. What about you? I suggest you brainstorm a big list of words that reflect your values. Start by asking yourself, "What is important to me?" To help with this you can find big lists of value words in my first book *Heartbreak, Healing and Happiness* within an exercise called 'My Pink Heart Print'. Alternatively, just google 'value words' and many sites contain long lists.

Once you have your own long list, try to reduce it slowly to the top twenty, then to the top ten and then to the top five. It can be a bit of a project to get to the top five, but once you have them you can apply them to all areas of your life so that you live in alignment with your true inner self.

Stop, take a deep breath and reflect. Give yourself permission to go inward, access your Inner Pink Star and the paw prints on your heart. Follow their lead all the way home to the pure, unconditional love of two souls connected as one, holding a love that never dies as you heal your loss, feel the love and appreciate the lessons, knowing that *the whole point is love!*

Honour yourself and your pet and record your feelings in your Pink Pet Grief Journal as you ponder the questions below.

- 🐾 What have I learnt about values?
- 🐾 What have I learnt from my pet about values?
- 🐾 What would be different in my life if I lived according to my top five values?

Contemplate and integrate this lesson while you move forward in your grief and your healing. You get a chance to design your life, unlike your furry friends. Visualise who and what you want your life to look like in order to get clarity on what you want. Then apply the values and go and live out that life with focus, purpose and motivation. You can learn a lot from Max and your pet as their list of values is always full of expression, purpose, meaning and love.

Presence

- *Max's Manifesto says: Be fully present in each moment. Begin to be mindful and in the flow as you enjoy and live each moment, embodying and uniting mind, body and spirit.*

Spiritual teacher and author Eckhart Tolle says, "If you are not living this moment, you are not really living". How does this resonate with you?

You only need to look at your feet and watch your furry friends as they romp around, oblivious to the past (with the exception of animals who have lived through trauma and may have behavioural issues) and not interested in the future, to see the truth in those words. All they care about is the present moment. A wag of their tail or a drop, wriggle and roll is what they are interested in as they live fully and joyfully in their body and their moment. We could learn so much, improve our health and reduce our stress levels enormously if we could adopt even a smidgen of their innate wisdom.

Adopt a new furry mantra: "The present moment is where life occurs."

Unfortunately, many of us worry so much about the future or ruminate about the past, not realising that we are slowly squandering our life away. Living this way sees us feeling every day more distracted and disconnected from our body, mind, heart and life. We forget to grasp that each moment is a small miracle that we are privileged to experience, be it good or bad.

Death teaches us that life can be over in a second. Life is short. Death teaches us to appreciate life and all that it offers. It teaches us that if we don't notice things, people and our environment – everything – RIGHT NOW, the moment may be gone forever. It's all about the experiences that change, shape and help us to grow. Each moment brings beautiful lessons and gifts. Despite grief bringing intense sorrow and sadness, it also brings delightful beauty and love. The key is being present and mindful.

Practising mindfulness, as explained earlier, is being present. It helps you to accept where you are in your life, be it a state of joy or a painful emotion. As humans we are exposed to both. It's just part of who we are and how we are put together. All states are temporary. One arises and soon it passes and another one arises. Nothing stays the same forever. We are always in a state of flux and flow.

Whichever state you are currently in, use mindfulness to just be with it instead of running away, living in denial or avoidance. By simply 'being', you can begin to move through the emotions and allow the energy of the emotion to rise to the surface, be felt, processed and exited from the body.

As a human you come with thoughts. You can't stop them. Like most of us, your thoughts control your mind, your emotions and then your actions and behaviours. A lot of your thoughts play out in your unconscious mind as an automatic thought without you even knowing it has arisen. Before you know it, you have been

Learnings from a Dog's Life: Max's Manifesto

hijacked by a negative thought pattern, taking you down the rabbit hole so to speak, and soon you begin to feel the negative emotions associated with it.

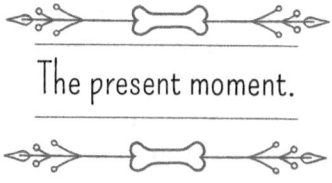

The present moment.

Mindfulness, however, is a productive way to settle your busy mind and brings many benefits. When you become more mindful and aware, you can consciously notice the thoughts as they arise, identify and acknowledge them without attachment or judgement, and then play the observation game while staying present. This allows you to choose to let them go before you are stuck deep in the rabbit hole. This has been my key for quietening the busy mind and relieving anxieties. Essentially, it is about witnessing, observing and being aware of your thoughts when they arise and then consciously making a choice to let them go and come back to the present moment.

To come back to the present moment, you use an anchor. This could be the breath, a mantra, counting or simply saying 'inhale' and 'exhale' as you breathe. Your meditation and mindfulness can be practised in stillness as you focus directly on your anchor. However, they can also be practised while you are in action. Any action really can bring you to the present.

Think about eating an apple using mindfulness. You pick the apple up and feel the texture, softness, smoothness and coolness of its skin. As you take that first bite, the tastebuds enjoy the sweetness and juiciness as it swirls around your mouth.

What about mindfulness when doing the dishes? You feel the warmth of the water on your hands and the shape and texture of the dish you are cleaning, being with the action in a state of openness and attention on being in the present.

Mindful people are said to be happier, more joyful, healthier, calmer, less stressed, less prone to anxiety and depression, and able to have happier relationships. Like anything, it takes practice to be mindful or meditate in stillness or in action. You can't do it once and expect to relieve all your anxiety and still all your chaotic thoughts. You need to make a small commitment to self to practise regularly. You only need to start small, maybe five minutes a day or every time you do the dishes. Pick an action or a time and see if you can incorporate it into your everyday routine.

Be like our furry friends. They can visit the park and sniff every leaf and piece of grass surrounding their favourite tree, meet new people and look for treats, scour the BBQ area for scraps, and continually live in joy and appreciation for each precious moment. They engage with everything and lose track of time. They live in the flow of life, wagging their tail at inconsequential things, wearing their big clown smile with utter joy. Just being. They don't follow a clock; they follow their heart and live a full life because of it.

So, maybe tomorrow, can you be a little more in the moment?

Delight in a simple walk, share some time with friends or family, relish the wind in your hair, savour the smell of jasmine in spring, appreciate the crash of the waves at the beach or even welcome the natter of conversation around the water cooler at work. Just be present in each moment and pay attention to your life. Ask what is happening around you. Then use your senses to listen, smell, touch, see and taste your way through it.

Turn off the devices and get excited and exhilarated, contemplate and ponder, relax and wonder. Be inquisitive and let go of the thoughts, surrendering to the moment. Don't let the opportunities of the present moment pass you by. The present moment quickly becomes the past and you may find yourself wallowing in it because you didn't appreciate it when you were in it. Or conversely you are worrying so much about the future moment you miss the magical moment that is here and now, right under your nose.

LEARNINGS FROM A DOG'S LIFE: MAX'S MANIFESTO

 ## PINK PET REFLECTIONS: PRESENCE

Stop, take a deep breath and reflect. Give yourself permission to go inward, access your Inner Pink Star and the paw prints on your heart. Follow their lead all the way home to the pure, unconditional love of two souls connected as one, holding a love that never dies as you heal your loss, feel the love and appreciate the lessons, knowing that *the whole point is love!*

Honour yourself and your pet and record your feelings in your Pink Pet Grief Journal as you ponder the questions below.

- 🐾 What have I learnt about the present moment?
- 🐾 What have I learnt from my pet about the present moment?
- 🐾 Do I live in the present moment?
- 🐾 If not, can I work towards being more present in each moment?
- 🐾 What would be different in my life if I was more present?

Contemplate and integrate this lesson while you move forward in your grief and your healing. Live every day like a new day and every moment like a new moment. As you heal your grief, begin to let go of the past. Hold on, trust and journey into the future as you live fully in each beautiful gifted moment that is presented. Accept and appreciate whatever that brings. If you forget how, just remember your loved one and follow the paw prints for guidance. Be like Max and stop and sniff everything. Our pets are experts at this lesson.

Purpose

🐾 *Max's Manifesto says: Seek and discover your purpose – the reason you are here – and what you have to offer the world. Once you have unearthed it, share it with those around you and begin to see the difference it makes in their life and your own.*

There's nothing like death and grief to have you questioning your purpose. It brings up the whole theme of purpose. Why am I here? Why was my pet here? Where have they gone? What were they here for? What am I going to live for now?

Dogs teach us about purpose. Their purpose to me, in no uncertain terms, is to teach us how to give and receive unconditional love. It's that simple! When Max woke up each morning, he was always excited and would race to me for a morning pat. He would hover around me for breakfast then sleep at my feet while I worked, showered or watched television. His loyalty also ensured he was always there even when I was on the toilet. He didn't want to miss a moment. I can't forget the huge emotional displays when I came home. Whether it was after being out for five minutes or five hours, the joyful response was the same every time. The nudging, the pawing, the big soppy eyes and the goofy clown smile. He was the embodiment of love. My loyal friend and fur child.

What do your pets do to display unconditional love and how do they live their purpose to teach you about love? Maybe they follow you around the house and up and down the hallway every time you move. Most always seem to be hot on our heels. Watch out if you turn around in a hurry as they are always there – a major tripping hazard. What is individual to your pet and your relationship? Maybe all dogs are not so needy like Max, but no doubt they show unconditional love in their own special heart-warming ways.

Learnings from a Dog's Life: Max's Manifesto

When I adopted my senior nanna Chelsea, I only had her for a few days and she had already stolen my heart. She had lived her purpose, practised her unique traits and wormed her way in so quickly. It was unconditional love all coming my way. Those eyes are the giveaway to the unconditional love that is shared between the two souls connected as one. Maybe she was channelling Max?

Grief opens our hearts and our minds and, in this opening and transformation, you may begin to question your purpose in life – this one life you get. And what a good question. To live your purpose is to live a full life with meaning.

I truly believe that each of us is put here on this Earth with specific purposes to fulfil. You have more talent, ability and potential than you give yourself credit for. Just look to your Inner Creator and what it highlighted for you. Pay attention and look deep within to your Inner Pink Star who is there to guide you. Seek further afield and you may just find it. The gift of your purpose is waiting to be unwrapped and delivered to the world, a world that will be all the better off because of you.

Living in the moment and noticing life is a good start to realising purpose. Once you have purpose in your life things begin to change quite dramatically. You begin to wake up with zest and vigour, jumping out of bed in eager anticipation for how the new day will unfold. Another day where you can paint with your talents and purpose. You become engaged in the flow of the moment, living and loving your dharma as the yogis say.

Everything begins to become aligned and feels right inside. Your inner self lights up so brightly, you feel purposeful, connected, useful and confident. You walk the earth with a skip in your step, lightly placing your feet on the earth as you manoeuvre through it.

Life is here to teach us. It's about growth and learning about ourselves and how we can become the best version of ourselves possible while accessing and enjoying inner peace and joy. Each of us deserves to be true and authentic to our deepest, heartfelt desires as we help ourselves and in turn help others.

To learn from life we need to put ourselves out there a little and takes chances and risks. Otherwise, we may start to feel like we are withering inside our comfort rut. This can be frightening and the thought of change overwhelming. I get it. I was there. I stood on the precipice of big change twice, and both times I eventually chose to dive right in!

In my experience, once you step out of the fear and into the love, into what is in your heart space, fear dissipates slowly and purpose evolves in front of you. Love is much stronger than fear. Your life changes wholeheartedly as does your purpose. You begin to manifest what your heart is calling for with things being presented for you. You begin to shed your old layers and negative patterns and walk in the positive footsteps your furry friends left behind.

When you are the ripe old age of 100 and reflect on your life, how do you want it to look? Do you want to look back with joy as having taken the risks that proved fruitful and changed your life remarkably for the better? Or not? If not, do you want fear to be the only thing that stood in your way?

False – Evidence – Appearing – Real = FEAR!

You are the author of your life. You get to design your life the way you choose. So you may need to make some different choices to turn your life around, and it may be like turning around the Titanic: a mammoth task. But it is so totally possible, and it all starts with one step.

Let's start with a mini assessment.

1. Do you have a sense of freedom, engagement, lightness and joy as you rise to each new day? With a smile and an appreciation for the wonder and beauty of life?

    or

Learnings from a Dog's Life: Max's Manifesto

2. Do you trudge through your days at work, waiting for the clock to strike five, feeling stressed, empty and a little soulless inside?

I'm hoping you feel number one. But for many I fear the answer may be number two.

There is a better way!

In theory, it's simple to find your purpose and live it. In reality, it is a little bit trickier to escape the rut and turn the Titanic in its new direction. But the easy bit is it just takes the first step. Awareness is that first step. Knowing you are not happy is the revelation that can turn you around and get you to start investigating other options.

Each of us is different. For one, a preferred new option might be to be a mum and bake the most delicious cakes and slices for their children to return home to after school. For another, it may be climbing up the corporate banking ladder. For others, it may be somewhere in the middle.

For me, it is all about DOGS – ITALY – YOGA – BOOKS! They all light up my world and my smile.

Whatever it is for you, just make sure it is authentic and comes from your heart space and not from the 'shoulds' via those around you. A key to finding your purpose may be found in your passions!

Commit to your world and your growth. Be more conscious, more awake, more aware. Know who you are, find your purpose and live 100 percent in alignment with it. How do you do that? You do what you love and what comes from your heart. Find your passions, always learn, try new things, stretch yourself, find your role models. Create a vision board and/or get a coach.

Awareness.

Whatever you do, appreciate the journey. Shake it up a bit. Dive deep. Do whatever it takes to fill your heart and your world with your purpose. When you live your purpose the universe smiles with you.

 ## Pink Pet Reflections: Purpose

Stop, take a deep breath and reflect. Give yourself permission to go inward, access your Inner Pink Star and the paw prints on your heart. Follow their lead all the way home to the pure, unconditional love of two souls connected as one, holding a love that never dies as you heal your loss, feel the love and appreciate the lessons, knowing that *the whole point is love!*

Honour yourself and your pet and record your feelings in your Pink Pet Grief Journal as you ponder the questions below.

- What have I learnt about purpose?
- What have I learnt from my pet about my purpose?
- Do I currently live my purpose?
- If not, would I like to live a more purposeful life?
- What would be different in my life if I was living my purpose?

Now look within your heart to see if you can settle your mind. Then answer these next questions directly from your heart space.

- What are my passions?
- What makes me feel alive, excited and enthused?
- What am I doing when I totally lose track of time?

Learnings from a Dog's Life: Max's Manifesto

- If I won the lottery, what would I do with my time?
- What excited me when I was a child?
- If I had only one year to live, what would I do?
- What does my heart tell me to do?
- When I look at others doing things, what am I envious of?
- What lights me up?
- What would I do even if I didn't get paid for it?

Now let's visualise for a moment!

Imagine there are two of you: yourself right now and a 110-year version of yourself. You are sitting silently opposite each other with a cup of tea, looking deeply into each other's eyes.

Take a moment to honour and appreciate this older version of yourself and all that you have been through. Settle in for a bit.

Then when you have become acquainted, allow your older self to give you some words of advice in helping you find your purpose and passions. What does she say? What pearls of wisdom is she waiting to tell you? Has she found the passions and implemented them into her life that you as yet have not seen come to fruition? Or is she disappointed, sad and unhappy for lack of trying? See if any epiphanies arrive for you.

Bring together all the questions above and this visualisation:

Can you now define and list the four to five things in your world that are your passions?

Start from there to derive your purpose and how you may integrate this into your daily life.

> Contemplate and integrate this lesson while you move forward in your grief and your healing. Investigate, read, research, study, volunteer, ask questions, be involved, find a role model... Just do whatever you need to do to incorporate more of these things in your life. It may start slowly, but the sooner you do more of what you love, the more you will love your life. Start somewhere and suddenly, opportunities will begin to open up. Take your furry friend's lead like I did with Max, and allow their wisdom and paw prints to lead you all the way to your purpose and then live the life they would want for you.

Feelings

🐾 *Max's Manifesto says: Allow all your rainbow of emotions to surface and be felt. Feel your feelings. Acknowledge and honour them as a part of who you are. Begin to befriend them, rather than run in avoidance, and notice the internal freedom you begin to experience.*

Each time your furry friends run to the door to greet you they are joyful. Then each time you leave and say, "I'll be back soon" they seem to express some sadness and mope a little. But generally they move through their feelings swiftly without assigning beliefs, values and thoughts to them. They don't get stuck in their emotions. They express and process them on the spot: no repression, no suppression. Once they are finished, they wag their tail all the way to their next nap or treat.

What about us? What can we learn from our furry friends?

As part of our human condition we are born with the whole spectrum of feelings and emotions. It is what differentiates us

Learnings from a Dog's Life: Max's Manifesto

from other species and what enables us to live a multifaceted life. A life with the bliss and beauty of love and the devastation and sadness of loss and sorrow.

You may call some feelings and emotions good and some negative, but they are all just feelings. If you shut down the feelings that you label as negative, you are also closing yourself off to the good emotions. So, it makes sense to learn how to acknowledge, appreciate and deal with all your feelings and emotions. Then, despite feeling intense sadness and sorrow, you will also be able to experience overwhelming happiness, joy and bliss.

Once you can acknowledge, accept and deal with the whole rainbow of emotions you can move through life a little more smoothly, accepting opportunities and taking risks as they arise. You know you can deal with whatever presents. Like your furry friends, you don't have to be stuck in your emotions. Instead of closing yourself off to life in fear of awakening feelings and emotions that you are unable to control or handle, you can be confident in knowing that you can handle anything life throws at you.

If you choose to remain in a fearful space, you live in a comfort zone filled with unhealthy distractions that make your world smaller and smaller as you fight to avoid and deny your feelings.

Joy, happiness and bliss.

Sometimes the terms 'emotions' and 'feelings' are used interchangeably. But there is a difference. Emotions precede feelings and are physical and instinctual, prompting instant bodily reactions. For example, when you see a long-lost friend you run up to them with excitement to give them a hug. Feelings, however, involve cognitive input and arise in the mind as a portrayal of what is happening in the physical body. They are sparked by emotions and coloured by personal experiences, beliefs, memories, values and thoughts that are linked to those emotions. Essentially, a feeling is your brain assigning a meaning to the emotion you are experiencing.

There is a lot of literature out there on feelings and emotions, and the commonly recognised core emotions are sadness, fear, anger, joy, surprise and disgust. Then there are many off-shoots – different variations – of each of these. So, it can be a minefield to manoeuvre around all of these, and it can do our emotional health a big disservice if we are unable to process them as they arrive.

We all know the benefit of good emotions; we feel nice. Generally, we find ourselves moving towards good ones and away from perceived negative ones at all costs. But there are also some benefits to the seemingly negative emotions if we deal with them positively such as:

- They help you get to know yourself better.
- They allow your body to be calmer once the negative energy is processed.
- They allow the blissful emotions to arise once the negative ones are released.
- They make you pay attention to what is happing in your life.
- They open up your mind to make some changes in your world.
- They bring clarity.
- They prepare you for difficult situations.
- They help you to learn how to problem-solve.
- They bring the opportunity for meditation and mindfulness.
- They release stored anxiety once processed.
- They help you to face your issues.
- They are your warning signs and guide you.

Learnings from a Dog's Life: Max's Manifesto

In processing, expressing and releasing your emotions, even the negative ones, you begin to unite your body, mind and spirit and make room for a whole host of beautiful warm emotions to radiate your being. Once this happens your world becomes a brighter and more amazing place. It's like you're wagging your tail again!

My little equation for helping you to deal with your emotions as we discovered early in this book goes like this: STOP, Be aware, Feel, Express, Heal.

Think about each time you have a good cry. At the end, once you are completely devoid of tears, often a euphoric sense comes over you. Once negative emotions stored in your body have been released, the blissful loving emotions that were waiting underneath are experienced.

To feel it is to process it. To process it is to express it. To express it is to start to heal it.

Yoga is a good tool to teach you to sit with your emotions and allow the energy to rise through your body and be released. Deeply held emotions can flow through you and make their way to the surface for release. Tears may accompany this, which you simply allow to flow. Leaving the mind open but not allowing it to judge or attach to the process sees the emotions releasing with less effort and complications.

Essentially, you are processing the emotions without allowing the feelings to get in the way. This is a process that takes time to learn, but yoga and meditation are a great start, even integrating them for just five or ten minutes into your day.

 Pink Pet Reflections: Feelings

Stop, take a deep breath and reflect. Give yourself permission to go inward, access your Inner Pink Star and the paw prints on your heart. Follow their lead all the way home to the pure, unconditional love of two souls connected as one, holding a love that never dies as you heal your loss, feel the love and appreciate the lessons, knowing that *the whole point is love!*

Honour yourself and your pet and record your feelings in your Pink Pet Grief Journal as you ponder the questions below.

- 🐾 What have I learnt about my feelings?
- 🐾 What have I learnt from my pet about my feelings?
- 🐾 Do I understand the benefit of processing and expressing my feelings?
- 🐾 Do I actually process and express my feelings?
- 🐾 What would be/is different in my life now that I can feel my feelings?

Contemplate and integrate this lesson while you move forward in your grief and your healing. Be aware of and explore your feelings. Honour and trust them. Feel your feelings and be honest with them. They are a part of you and avoiding the negative will only see your life shrinking in front of you. Allowing them all to be felt will be the biggest gift you can give yourself. An amazingly rich and full life will follow. Max asks that you give yourself this gift.

LEARNINGS FROM A DOG'S LIFE: MAX'S MANIFESTO

TRUTH AND AUTHENTICITY

🐾 *Max's Manifesto says: Be authentic, where you can stand solidly on the earth with an intimate knowledge of who you are and what you need and desire. Allow all the beautiful individual parts of yourself to shine and be expressed to the world.*

Being authentic is being real, genuine, original and individual. There is no room for falsity or copying.

I don't know any being that is more authentic and truer to themselves than dogs. Even when they do put on an act (and let's face it, they can put on acts and try to twist us around their paws to get their favourite treat), it is so obvious, and still they are so cute. They are so genuine, each having their own personality.

Dogs don't feel peer pressure or worry about what others think. They don't care about the latest fashions, how they woof to each other, which tree they pee on, how they greet the mailman or which career they pursue – couch potato or treat sniffer – they just be themselves and act accordingly. It is so simple and beautifully authentic!

In this observation is a lesson that your pet can teach you, which can be wildly life-changing if you give yourself permission to become your true and authentic self. It is also a lesson from the grief process. As you grieve your heart opens and a domino effect begins. You start to trust and honour your heart and transform yourself to live more authentically, not just in your grief journey but your whole life.

It takes a lot of energy and stress to live an unauthentic life, and when you are in grief, you don't have that extra energy. Sometimes all you have is enough energy to survive. So, often grief allows you to stop and reflect on your need to act in a more authentic way.

Loss, Love and Lessons

Do you always exist as your magnificent authentic self? The you that makes you? The you that is different from everyone else that silently begs to be expressed to the world? Perhaps it's the you that dances crazily in your pyjamas or sings loudly in the shower when no one is around. There is only one you and the world deserves the full expression of that you. So this is an important question to ponder.

If you don't know what that looks like, begin your inner quest to seek and dig deeply until you discover what your truth looks like. Then make a choice – a most sacred intention – to live this every day.

Living your truth furnishes your life with a sense of solidness, gratification and serenity. You will find life calmer and more peaceful and joyful as you radiate a simple happiness of the self. The difference between living a life of truth versus living in an inauthentic space can be astonishing. It is generally easily recognisable when you see it in others.

Living to please others all the time, and ensuring we escape ridicule, rejection or being alone, sees us repressing our self. We don't want to be the black sheep, so we follow along and mimic the rest of the crowd. Stress trails us as we battle strongly to keep our true self inside.

For a moment think about the individualists, the ones you may laugh at as they live outside the normal sphere. Maybe they dance solo on the dance floor, looking a little strange. Or they are an obvious stand-out due to their difference... whatever it may be. Maybe they are the courageous ones and don't fear acting differently. They let their true self hang out for all to see. I would suspect that if you spoke to them, they would be feeling calm and happy and not worrying what others think as they dance the night away.

Living unaligned to your truth and in suppression of self opens the door that allows anxiety, depression and a simple unhappiness to sneak in and infect your body, mind and heart. Living a life trying to please others, scared to say no and afraid to be an individual in fear of humiliation only confines you and your quirky nature to the boundaries of your skin and keeps you all locked up inside. Only you hold the key!

Dogs know differently. They will do a butt wiggle, dance at the park, make silly faces and loud bizarre noises, do a psycho run and fall over, sniff each other's behinds and allow themselves to be dressed up in crazy costumes. They never complain and don't care what others think. They just do and are true to themselves. They do in the moment what feels right to them, expressing their true nature.

Yes, they break the rules sometimes and steal food, dig up the garden and pee on inappropriate things. Then they skip merrily away to the next pat on the head. Yes, they try to please us continuously, but they do it all truthfully and with cheery joie de vivre.

Each dog is an individual and has their own character traits that we take joy in. We love that they are distinctive and take pride in their peculiarities, telling unending stories to others about their adventures. Why not be proud of your own peculiarities and, for that matter, the peculiarities of your friends and family? The world is a kaleidoscope of individuals shining their unique light.

Be authentic.

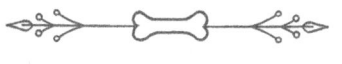

Our furry friends are generally very good at asking for what they want. They bark for attention, deliver a downward dog to initiate play, hover light-footedly near the treat jar when they feel hungry, nudge you to get your attention, and so on. Generally, in each moment they just respond with their truth.

As humans we are not good at communication and asking for what we want, often fearing rejection and losing love. We often place our worthiness on what others think of us and use their love to fill our inner voids. If we can learn assertion instead of aggression or passiveness, and value self-love and being authentic, we can learn to ask unapologetically for what is best for us. Just like our dogs, who we train to stay and take food gently, we can train ourselves to act assertively to get what we want without aggression.

We can concurrently learn to accept rejection as we know it's better to honour the self first, even if others don't like it. Also, if someone does not act in our best interests or fulfil our expectations regarding how we want to be treated, we learn to accept that maybe they are not the best person to be investing our time in. We begin to place more importance on self-love than grasping at external love from others. When we are with the right people, we can ask for our truth and it will be delivered gracefully, or at least declined and discussed maturely and respectfully.

The same goes for saying no. There is a big stigma about saying no and letting others down. But what about letting yourself down? Which is more important?

Do you ever say yes when you mean no? Maybe to a friend who asks you to go to the pictures or dinner when you are exhausted and unwell? This yes is given to the detriment to your health. If they are truly a great friend, they will totally understand. Wouldn't you if the situation was in reverse?

Sometimes it's a bigger scenario. Have you said yes to a career path or a job to please others when you wished you could say no? Perhaps even your whole soul was silently screaming for you to take a different path better suited to you. Your yes was given to the detriment of your career and your wellbeing and may have led to more anxiety and stress.

Where you are at in your life in this precise moment is largely brought about from your past decisions to say yes or no. Of course, in some dire situations like abuse, you may at certain points have experienced that your right to say your own yes

LEARNINGS FROM A DOG'S LIFE: MAX'S MANIFESTO

without your conscious knowledge was taken away. You may feel you haven't made certain choices and things have just happened to you. Maybe you said more yes's than no's. However, sometimes not saying no was a choice that helped to lead you to where you reside today. But it's never too late to learn when to say yes and when to say no and that it is in your best interest to design the life you want. It's now a matter of returning to your newfound self-love and taking responsibility for your life.

Sometimes this is a big lesson but the beauty of this is that all you need to do now if you are not happy is to say yes to life and maybe a few no's to some things or people. Make a different choice, author and build your new life and butt wiggle all the way to your new happiness.

A few tips to find your authenticity:

- Accept who you are, your strengths and your areas for improvement.
- Be your quirky self.
- Support yourself with self-love.
- Love others unconditionally.
- Walk away if someone comprises your true self.
- Allow yourself to change and grow.
- Trust your Inner Pink Star.
- Express your thoughts, feelings and views.
- Be attuned to your feelings and act according and appropriately.
- Be honest and impeccable with your word.
- Be assertive instead of aggressive or passive.
- Listen attentively to others rather than always offering advice.
- Treat others with kindness and respect.

Loss, Love and Lessons

- 🐾 Live in the moment.
- 🐾 Drop the people-pleasing.
- 🐾 Remove the comparison game.
- 🐾 Don't blame others.
- 🐾 Take responsibility for your life.
- 🐾 Enjoy and share your sense of humour.
- 🐾 Only look to yourself for your approval, not others.
- 🐾 Be happy when others succeed.
- 🐾 Remove attachment and judgement.
- 🐾 Be open to learning from your mistakes.
- 🐾 Don't take life so seriously.
- 🐾 Make your own decisions.
- 🐾 Say no more often and yes only when you truly mean it.
- 🐾 Ride the waves of the breath in the physical body.
- 🐾 Value life over material possessions.

So, listen to your Inner Pink Star, your inner guide. Like Max would have, follow your nose to the prize – in this case, your truth – and bark it out loud. Your true self resides deep within and needs a little digging up just like the bone buried deep in the earth that your furry friend scurries to dig up and claim.

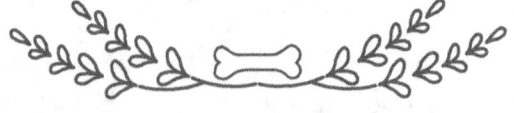

 ## Pink Pet Reflections: Truth

Stop, take a deep breath and reflect. Give yourself permission to go inward, access your Inner Pink Star and the paw prints on your heart. Follow their lead all the way home to the pure, unconditional love of two souls connected as one, holding a love that never dies as you heal your loss, feel the love and appreciate the lessons, knowing that *the whole point is love!*

Honour yourself and your pet and record your feelings in your Pink Pet Grief Journal as you ponder the questions below.

- What have I learnt about truth and authenticity?
- What have I learnt from my pet about truth and authenticity?
- Can I integrate truth and authenticity into my being and my life?
- What is holding me back from being more authentic?
- What would be different in my life if I could be more truthful and authentic?

Contemplate and integrate this lesson while you move forward in your grief and your healing. Max says with a big woof that your Inner Pink Star always knows what is best for you and will take you on the cherished path of building a truthful and authentic life. You just need to stop and listen to her and the outstanding advice she offers.

Fun

 Max's Manifesto says: Lastly, have some FUN!

Someone important once said to me, "Lara, don't take life so seriously". Words of great wisdom from a modern-day sage and ones that I contemplate over and over. Boy, do our pets teach us this one also!

Our furry friends have a marvellous way of displaying fun. They drop, wriggle and roll, doing a little dance on their back on the green grass. They run off to the creek and get covered in mud. They sniff the butts of every dog they meet and run and chase them around the park. They just engage with everything in the moment, bringing immense joy to their lives and ours. If they could laugh, I am sure they would be laughing all the time except for when they were eating, sleeping or pooping.

Now I'm trying to imagine what a doggy laugh would sound like, and I realise for me that's a moment of fun because it has brought a big smile to my face. Now in my mind materialises the laughter of Muttley, Penelope Pitstop's friend from *Wacky Races* (the Hanna-Barbera cartoon TV series that started in the late 1960s). His crazy laugh is echoing in my ears as I realise just how silly I am being. Aha... I remember that's what fun is all about. (For a good laugh, search YouTube for Muttley's laugh and you'll know what I'm talking about!)

When we are children we can be like our furry friends. We run around, do silly things, listen to our hearts, don't worry what others think, are true to ourselves, place fun first, get dirty in the sandpit, raise our voices in laughter and fall asleep at the end of the day after a fun-filled day. Essentially, children live life with little or no stress and a body, mind and soul that is united, living in the present moment and filled with joy.

LEARNINGS FROM A DOG'S LIFE: MAX'S MANIFESTO

So what happens as we get older? Well, the human condition gets layered over us with:

- others' expectations
- the desire to fit in
- the need to be responsible
- the pressures to survive
- the need to feel important
- the need to earn a living
- a desire to climb the corporate or social ladder
- modern-day distractions from our true self
- the pleaser in us
- the ability to only say yes when we mean no
- the comparison game we play with others
- our achievement junkie side
- perfectionist traits
- the burnout road
- the exhaustion, overwhelm, boredom and comfort rut
- our worries.

… and so many other things that get embedded in our personality as we grow and age.

Do any of these sound familiar? Don't you feel overwhelmed just reading them all? It's no wonder fun gets pushed to the bottom of the list.

Research shows that adding more fun to your life can increase your productivity at work, improve your health, boost your happiness and improve your relationships. Fun is a gift to a happier, more enjoyable life. It's really so obvious!

When was the last time you laughed till you cried? When you had so much fun you got totally lost in the moment? Ask yourself if it is time to bring some of this back into your life. Do you hear a resounding YES?

So, get honest with yourself, and if you agree you need more fun in your life, you can start planning. Firstly, it's important to realise the benefits of fun and to move it a little higher to the top of your priority list and values in life. What you value in your life generally affects how you live your days out. But you have to deeply value it, truly desiring this to emerge.

Visualise fun in whatever form that means to you and, as you do, you will begin to manifest it into being. Make a big list of all the things that used to bring fun to you, then add to your list more fun things you would like to try. List what makes you laugh. Sometimes it is the simple things like tickle fights with your children or sometimes it's bigger like a vacation. Just find what fun means to you personally.

Begin to schedule time for fun! While you are busy being busy in your day, stop for a moment and check in to see if you have had any fun today. Just like when you ask yourself if you have had enough water to drink today, ask yourself if you have had enough fun. And ask often. Change your perception a little around what is important in your life.

When you are old and unwell and thinking back on your life, what will you remember? I know for me it will be the moments spent with my loved ones and the laughter and joy we shared and the fun times we had. It will definitely not be the list of things I had to do today, which I no doubt will not even remember in the slightest.

So let's remember what our pets teach us. We can really learn a lot from them around fun, and I am sure they will be more than willing to be your furry wingman on the fun journey. Why not start by committing each day to take your doggy to the park and just observe. Let them teach you how to bring some fun into your life. Listen, observe and learn. Allow some of their cheekiness and naughtiness to colour your life and with it will flow enthusiasm, curiosity and adventure.

 ## Pink Pet Reflections: Fun

Stop, take a deep breath and reflect. Give yourself permission to go inward, access your Inner Pink Star and the paw prints on your heart. Follow their lead all the way home to the pure, unconditional love of two souls connected as one, holding a love that never dies as you heal your loss, feel the love and appreciate the lessons, knowing that *the whole point is love!*

Honour yourself and your pet and record your feelings in your Pink Pet Grief Journal as you ponder the questions below.

- What have I learnt about fun?
- What have I learnt from my pet about having fun?
- Do I understand the benefits of play and fun in my life?
- Do I actually allow time for fun?
- What would be different if I had more fun?

Contemplate and integrate this lesson while you move forward in your grief and your healing. Face your fears, live life, laugh uncontrollably, take up the new hobby, meet lots of people, write a little less on your to-do lists, schedule fun, sniff out the smiles, wag your behind on the road to new things, hang out with friends who will join your fun escapade, stick your head out the window and feel the breeze on your face. Follow your nose and choose life with fun as one of your top values and be like your furry friend. In this lesson they really are the teacher and have all the answers. As Max knows, if you follow this recipe, before you know it you will be immersed in FUN!

Lessons contemplations

It is unfortunate that our furry friends live such short lives where we most likely outlive them. Each pet we love brings us loss, love and lessons in both their living and in their passing. Each brings us something different and possibly even leads us to a new way of being.

Know that all types of grief leave us with lessons on our heart. All types of grief transform each of us individually in some way. Create awareness and notice what is happening internally. My observation is that they teach us to live life fully and especially to do the following:

- 🐾 Give and receive unconditional love – the most beautiful kind of love where no limitations or conditions are placed and you can be your beautiful self.

- 🐾 Be self-loving and live in the peaceful place where you continually grow physically, mentally, emotionally and spiritually. Where you know, honour and accept all parts of yourself.

LEARNINGS FROM A DOG'S LIFE: MAX'S MANIFESTO

- 🐾 Live a healthy life physically, mentally, emotionally and spiritually. Make sure you eat a varied healthy diet, exercise routinely, and sleep well to heal and restore your body. In general, consider all aspects of a healthy life that lead you to your own homeostasis, that is, balance.

- 🐾 Unearth your values and live by them every day. List your top five and see if you are truly living by them. Where there are some gaps see what you can do differently to begin to transform your life.

- 🐾 Be fully present in each moment. Begin to be mindful and in the flow as you enjoy and live each moment, embodying and uniting mind, body and spirit.

- 🐾 Seek and discover your purpose – the reason you are here – and what you have to offer the world. Once you have unearthed it, share it with those around you and begin to see the difference it makes in their life and your own.

- 🐾 Allow all your rainbow of emotions to surface and be felt. Feel your feelings. Acknowledge and honour them as a part of who you are. Begin to befriend them, rather than run in avoidance, and notice the internal freedom you begin to experience.

- 🐾 Be authentic, where you can stand solidly on the earth with an intimate knowledge of who you are and what you need and desire. Allow all the beautiful individual parts of yourself to shine and be expressed to the world.

- 🐾 Lastly, have some FUN!

So many lessons! So much wisdom! So much love!

Appreciate the lessons!

Loss, Love and Lessons

"If you have a dog, you will most likely outlive it; to get a dog is to open yourself to profound joy and, prospectively, to equally profound sadness."

—Marjorie Garber

Epilogue

> "A good dog never dies."
>
> —Mary Carolyn Davies

I write the epilogue to this book as Suzy, my twelve-year-old golden retriever, Princess Chelsea, my sixteen-year-old Labrador and Pippy, my brand new ten-week-old golden retriever, sit at my feet patiently waiting for dinner. It's about 5.20pm, only about ten minutes before Chelsea gets really agitated. I can run the clock by her stomach. It never misses a beat.

What a perfect moment. To live in this moment forever, where my senior and junior fur children are here, healthy and happy, just hanging out with me forever. That would be perfect! But I know this will not be the case. I know they have short lives and that in the not-too-distant future, I will need to say goodbye once again. I cry as I write, not only because I have been drawn out of the moment and feel sad about what has not even happened yet, but because the love is so deep. I know the loss will devastate me again.

The deeper the love, the deeper the grief. This dichotomy once again highlights to me the beauty of the love and the devastation of the grief.

But I would not have it any other way. I want to love as deeply as I can, which means I need to accept that I will grieve just as deeply.

Loss, Love and Lessons

If I am to parent more furry children, I will need to walk to the centre of the pain to walk out the other side towards the love over and over again. I am okay with that! This is what I have done for Max, and what I will do for Suzy, Chelsea and Pippy and any other fur children that come into my life when it is time to say our final goodbyes.

My life has once again been transformed by grief, by my loss of Max, by my love for Max, and by the lessons that Max leaves me. I have healed my loss and grief yet allow it to live assimilated inside me just as Max is. I have felt the love so deeply and I appreciate the lessons every day.

Max came into the world as an adorable, cute puppy with a sole purpose to love me unconditionally. He modelled this to me for his entire life to teach me how to also love unconditionally. He served his purpose up on a silver platter and made it so easy for me to absorb this lesson because the love was so raw, perfect, pure and deep.

He gifted me many more lessons in his short life as I have shared with you, and they have all had a profound effect on who I am today and how I live my life. I am perpetually blessed to have had Max as my fur baby to shower with love and affection and basically spoil him rotten in return. Because that is what he deserved.

I believe saying goodbye is not the end despite how difficult it is. It is just another beginning; a new way of life where Max is no longer at my feet or forever waiting at the gate for me with his clown smile but instead, like an exquisite oil painting, his paw prints are beautifully painted all over my heart and leading the way forward with love.

The paw prints softly reside there. Some days they bring tears, sometimes laughter, sometimes just memories. But every time they bring love as they take me on this journey forward. My heart fiercely treasures, protects and nourishes this precious love. Through this love, Max helps me to materialise a life full of love,

Epilogue

laughter, lessons, many fur children at my feet and tumbleweeds of fur throughout my house.

Living in your grief is difficult until you realise you are also living in your love – the love of you and your fur child. It is always accessible. It can bring loss, it can bring love and it can bring lessons. Allow it to deliver all three and see your life grow and deepen as you experience the full spectrum of your emotions, your feelings and your life. Understand that without grief there is no love. Use your courage and strength to walk the grief journey and discover the lessons that emerge and the inner transformation that takes place.

Through *Loss, Love and Lessons* you have learnt how to heal your loss, feel the love and appreciate the lessons. Let's review what you learnt.

In *Part 1 The Loss* you read Max's story and my story of loss, with my hope that reading our stories helped you to connect to your own. I took you through all the steps leading up to, and soon after, Max's passing, which may have answered some questions circling your mind about your own situation. I hope it gave you some peace of mind knowing that others have been through the same journey you are now walking. Knowing others got through it may bring some hope that you can too. It just takes some time, some work and some patience.

You also learnt more about how grief works, to permit grief to have a voice, what role society plays and why pet grief cuts so deep. It is often a misunderstood journey and I hope this section helped to make more sense of it for you to heal the loss.

In *Part 2 The Love*, you learnt to process and express your grief and to transform through your grief all the way to the pure love awaiting you at the end of the journey. You learnt more about the raw grief and why it hurts so much. You explored the human-animal bond and the beautiful unconditional love. You then moved onto the grief models and learnt about the stages of grief and how they can help you and your children process and express your grief to unearth the love. You were equipped with loving tools and strategies and numerous different ways to process your grief with a love-grief toolbox. From there, you looked at creating a personal memorial, tribute and eulogy for your pet. Lastly, you learnt about when it may be time to get a new pet. Essentially, this part was about following the paw prints and journeying deeply through the grief to the gift of love that awaits you on the other side so you can feel the love.

In *Part 3 The Lessons* you consolidated the beautiful lessons your pet gifts you in life and on their passing, and how you can learn and grow from your loss. You can now implement some of the simplistic lessons that your dog models to you. By appreciating these beautiful lessons it's wise to take them and assimilate them gently into your life where you feel they fit. The rewards from implementing these lessons from your furry friends will powerfully reside deep in your heart and transform how you live as you appreciate the lessons.

To reiterate, the overall themes you covered and the aim of my message are for you to:

- journey through the heartfelt loss and grief
- follow the loving paw prints made by your pet on your heart to the deep love within
- know that two souls are connected as one, holding a love that never dies
- heal your loss, feel the love and appreciate the lessons, knowing that *the whole point is love!*

Without grief there is no love. Allow yourself to walk the road of grief, to embrace the lessons and to welcome the beautiful gift of love that appears as you near the latter part of your grief journey.

EPILOGUE

Throughout you may still feel shrouded in grief. That is normal. It takes time and work to process your grief and you need to honour yourself through this journey. As you process the grief you will heal the loss, feel the love and appreciate the lessons. As you assimilate the lessons, allow internal changes to surface. Then let go and surrender to the new you that will arise from your grief due to these lessons. Give permission for yourself to blossom.

Look deep into your heart and know your furry friend is still right beside you. To remember your fur child now all you need to do is look deep within, find some stillness and wait for the paw prints to appear that will walk you home to the unconditional love in your heart.

Know that you are two souls connected as one, holding a love that never dies and that *the whole point is love!* This love is so deep that it cracks your heart wide open, which enables you to remember your furry friend and touch daily the love that shines down brightly from your angel across the Rainbow Bridge. When the time is right, this love may also wish to be shared and will possibly guide you to welcome more furry friends and more unconditional love into your life, just as I have done with Pippy joining our family. She will never replace Max, but the shared love between Max and I will multiply in this new relationship.

I wish the same for you.

Lara Casanova x

LOSS, LOVE AND LESSONS

Pink Pet Love Note

I love you, Max. Goodbye for now. I'll see you at Rainbow Bridge one day. Have fun but please don't wait at the gate...

The whole point is love!

Thanks for Reading My Book

Thank you for reading my book!

I appreciate all your feedback, and
I love hearing what you have to say.

I would really love your input to help make my future books better.

Please leave me a helpful review on Amazon, letting me know what you thought of the book.

A big PINK Thank you!

Lara Casanova

Appendix

Meditations

Short Meditation

Using the knowledge you have obtained from this book, you may like to follow the steps below to practise a quiet and simple introduction to meditation exercise. Meditation will help you to feel connected to yourself and your pet as you begin to open your heart. It is also an opportunity to celebrate your pet's life and your cherished memories. If you already have a regular practice, remember the benefits it brings and try to maintain your practice through this fragile and sorrowful time.

Stop, take a deep breath and reflect. Give yourself permission to go inward to access your Inner Pink Star and the paw prints on your heart. Follow their lead all the way home to the pure, unconditional love of two souls connected as one, holding a love that never dies as you heal your loss, feel the love and appreciate the lessons, knowing that *the whole point is love!*

Sit comfortably in a chair or on the ground with your legs crossed, spine elongated and softly close your eyes. Give yourself permission to receive and embrace the silence that resides within.

Bring your hands to the prayer position (Anjali mudra) in front of your heart, acknowledging the start of your meditation and representing honour, respect and love for yourself and your pet. Then allow the back of your hands to rest on your knees.

Once you are comfortable and have your eyes closed, begin:

- Welcome yourself to meditation.
- Feel the contact points on the chair or ground.
- Observe your breath.
- Inhale through your nose to a count of 1 – 2 – 3 – 4.
- Pause and hold the inhale for a count of 1 – 2 – 3 – 4.
- Exhale through your nose for a count of 1 – 2 – 3 – 4 – 5 – 6.
- Repeat. (Feel free to change the count of the breath. The aim is to make the exhalation longer than the inhalation to induce calm.)
- Allow yourself to softly fall into a deep, relaxed state.
- Once you have settled through your breathing, scan through the body to observe any tightness or tension and allow your breath to be directed to these areas to soften and release any tension.
- Once you are in this space you can begin to recall memories of your pet. Allow compassion, healing and love to flow through you.

APPENDIX

- If the exercise creates anxiety or stress, just remain with the breathing and come out of the meditation if necessary.
- When you are ready to come out of the meditation, bring your focus back to the breath – notice and observe. Then bring your focus back to the contact points on the chair or ground beneath you.
- When you are ready, slowly open your eyes to come out of the meditation.
- Contemplate your experience and feel gratitude for the time you spent with you.
- Record your feelings in your Pink Pet Grief Journal.

LONG MEDITATION

- Welcome yourself to your meditation.
- Feel the contact points on the chair or ground.
- Notice the physical body and encourage it to release any tension. Surrender and let go to any gripping.
- Notice the mental body and the thoughts, again beginning to release any attachment and judgements. Just be with them.
- Notice your emotional body and how you are feeling. Know that all emotions are energy that needs to flow through the body and all are temporary. See if you can just allow what is to be.

- 🐾 Now, notice your breathing. Is it deep, shallow, fast or slow? Simply observe.
- 🐾 Now, seat the breath deep into the lower abdominals in the belly region, noticing the belly rise on the inhale and fall on the exhale. Simply observe.
- 🐾 Begin to fill up the entire lung space with your breath. Inhale as you feel the lower abdominals rise then continue up to expand the rib cage outwards and then fill the upper chest.
- 🐾 Initiate the exhale from the lower abdominals first then the rib cage then the upper chest.
- 🐾 Continuing to breathe, creating a wave-like motion throughout the body as the breath moves through you.
- 🐾 Notice the pauses between the breaths, the rhythm of the breath, the whisper of the breath, the texture and temperature as the breath comes in and out through the nostrils, and the wave-like motion and oscillation throughout the body.
- 🐾 Continue to put all your focus on your breathing:
    - 🐾 As you inhale, say in your mind 'inhale'.
    - 🐾 As you exhale, say in your mind 'exhale'.
- 🐾 As a random thought enters your mind, acknowledge it and then let it drift away, coming back to your focus on the breath.
- 🐾 Continue to allow yourself to observe and witness the thoughts and then let them go, without attachment.
- 🐾 Continue to inhale and exhale.
- 🐾 Maintain the connection to your breath throughout the meditation as you open yourself to discover more on your inward journey.

APPENDIX

- When you are ready to come out of your meditation, bring your hands back to Anjali mudra in prayer at the heart centre. Acknowledge your inward journey and the honouring of self once again. Take a small bow by lowering your head to your heart and your heart to the earth.
- Sitting tall once again, wiggle your toes and fingers and bring your concentration back to the moment.
- Rub your hands together to create energy and place them over your closed eyes. Slowly open your eyes into the safe space and, when you are ready, remove your hands from your eyes to unite the internal and external world.
- Contemplate your experience and feel gratitude for the time you spent with you.
- Record your feelings in your Pink Pet Grief Journal.

Life in the Pink

Through my work at In the Pink I aim to radiate healthy vibrations into the world through positive writings, powerful consultations, yoga teachings and heartfelt services for those aiming to walk to a rich life full of love, truth and purpose.

Life in the Pink helps you learn how to travel and transform through your difficult journeys in life, facing your fears, heartbreaks and grief, bringing you home to a Life in the Pink. I hope to help you unearth your true self and inner wisdom that leads you to know, understand, nurture and love yourself. I wish to help you to travel on your journey in life feeling alive, rich and full, choosing to live authentically in following your soul's desire and life purpose.

I genuinely know it is possible to dig deep to find the love that is buried below the pain. It's there; trust me! Sometimes it just takes a while to find it and allow it to flourish. When you find it, and you will, it grants you the ability to feel strong, joyful and happy. Accessing all your love buried deep below and bringing it to the surface will allow you to become one with it and shine it out to your loved ones and everyone you meet.

Using your traumatic experiences as a learning tool and a gift can help to springboard you to a new life full of deep richness and joy. Acknowledge that you need patience, allow heartbreak and grief to pave your path, don't repress or suppress, be open to everything, remain strong and brave, keep your loved one alive in your heart and just *be!*

Services

Positive writings

Heartbreak, Healing and Happiness – Flourishing after a heartbreak. 2015

Allow me to accompany you on the journey through Heartbreak via Healing and arriving home flourishing in Happiness. Share in a comforting array of self-loving insights and tools, plus my very own raw personal experiences. Use the practical activities and exercises to help move you through the pain and suffering.

Redesign and redecorate your life and heal any old lingering hurts forever. Emerge feeling healed and happy with oodles of energy, eager to embark on your new, fun and exciting life adventure.

Heartbreak – Learn how to pick yourself up, transform through the grieving process, benefit from the lessons and create self-love.

Healing – Unearth your true self and inner wisdom. Befriend your inner critic and learn how to live a truly authentic life.

Happiness – Expose, design and chase your passions, create your vision, map your goals and start living your soul's desire and life purpose.

Flourish and live your individual version of happily ever after.

Heartbreak, Healing and Happiness is my first book and is available at local bookstores and most online stores. You can find more details on the Life in the Pink website.

LIFE IN THE PINK

GRIEF, GRACE AND GRATITUDE – TRANSFORMING THROUGH YOUR GRIEF JOURNEY. 2018

A beautiful love story, yours and the author's, walking together on the journey through Grief, Grace and Gratitude. Opening yourself to an understanding of grief will open your heart to heal. Opening your heart to heal ultimately opens your heart to love again. Walk through the stages of grief and return home to your true nature with a zealous desire to live a rich and full life in your loved one's honour.

Grief – Trek through the raw grief, surrendering to the twists and turns of the grief journey, taking you straight to the love in your heart.

Grace – Nurture yourself, prioritise your wants and needs, grow your self-love, follow your yearnings and unearth your truth.

Gratitude – Reap the rewards of your grief journey and shine in the gratitude of your loved one's life, enjoying the freedom to walk towards your life purpose.

Grief, Grace and Gratitude is my second book and is also available at local bookstores and most online stores as a paperback or an eBook. You can find more details on the Life in the Pink website.

PINK STORIES BLOG

Be inspired and informed through my Pink Stories blog on the Life in the Pink website.

ECOURSES

Continue to walk through your healing via my eCourses on the Life in the Pink website.

Yoga teachings

Join me in a Hatha flow yoga class to nurture, nourish and heal your body, mind and spirit. Class timetable and special events' details are listed on the Life in the Pink website.

Powerful one-on-one consultations

I am available by appointment for consultations to assist you with transforming your life. Email me through the Life in the Pink website.

Join my community

Subscribe to my blog/newsletter at the Life in the Pink website and receive a free eBook *Life in the PINK*. I will keep you updated monthly with the happenings at Life in the Pink.

Like my Facebook page and access daily inspirational, meaningful and fun reminders on how to live a Life in the Pink.

Join me on Instagram for more colourful inspiration.

Thank you so much for allowing Life in the Pink into your heart. I wish you always a beautiful Life in the Pink. I would love you to stay in touch and share your stories:

Web: www.lifeinthepink.com.au

Email: lara@lifeinthepink.com.au

Facebook: www.facebook.com/InthePINKxx/

Instagram: www.instagram.com/lifeinthepinkxx

Live in the love, truth and purpose.

Lara x

Acknowledgements

> "Such short little lives our pets have to spend with us, and they spend most of it watching for us to come home each day."
>
> —John Grogan

So many people have helped and supported me as I wrote this book and as I journey through life. I am truly blessed and grateful to have my people around me every day. Without our tribe beside us we cannot soar. Here are a few I would like to mention:

My immediate family – Dad (deceased), Mum, my sisters Dail, Becky and Nicole, Pat and my adorable nieces, Samantha, Charlie, Chloe, Imogen, Anna and Claire. Family, you are everything. I love you all.

My extended family – my aunties and uncles and all my wonderful cousins.

My late family – especially my dad and my grandparents and the generations that lived before me.

My friends – such a great circle of loving and fun people. Especially to Gemma and Anna.

Loss, Love and Lessons

All the people from Author Support Services who brought my third book to life.

Dr Katrina Warren for contributing the foreword for this book.

All my mentors and authors who have helped transform my life.

Suzy, Chelsea and Pippy, my three fur children who bring immense love and joy to my life.

Billy, Murray, Spikey and Kaly, thank you for being Max's best furry friends I hope you are all inseparable and playing at Rainbow Bridge.

Lastly but very importantly, Max. My main man. You left a zillion paw prints on my heart!

Thank you.

Extra Resources

Books

My theories and ideas are collated from my journey of many years of study, reading and personal experience. I have been privileged to find many mentors, as well as resources from others in my field. Here are publications from some of the most influential mentors and authors I have come across to date. Some are related to pet loss and grief while others are general in their nature but full of life wisdom. They will provide additional inspirational and soul-provoking reads to expand your spiritual healing and journey to amazing heights.

Ahlers, A. (2011). *Big Fat Lies Women Tell Themselves: Ditch your inner critic and wake up your inner superstar.* New World Library.

Ahlers, A., & Arylo, C. (2015). *Reform Your Inner Mean Girl: 7 steps to stop bullying yourself and start loving yourself.* Atria Books/Beyond Words.

Arylo, C. (2012). *Madly in Love with ME: The daring adventure of becoming your own best friend.* New World Library

Arylo, C. (2009). *Choosing ME Before WE: Every woman's guide to life and love.* New World Library.

Avanti, M. Daniel, S & Bocker's Mom. (2011). *Chasing Bocker's Tale.* First Edition Publishing.

Beak, S. (2013). *Red Hot and Holy: A heretic's love story.* 1st edition. Sounds True.

Behrendt, G. (2006). *It's Called a Break-Up Because It's Broken: The smart girl's breakup buddy.* Harper Element.

Bernstein, G. (2012). *Spirit Junkie: A radical road to self-love and miracles.* Harmony.

Bernstein, G. (2014). *Miracles Now: 108 life-changing tools for less stress, more flow, and finding your true purpose.* New York Times bestseller edition. Hay House, Inc.

Bernstein, G. (2011). *Add More ~Ing to Your Life: A hip guide to happiness.* Harmony.

Brathen, R. (2015). *Yoga Girl.* Touchstone.

Burchett, D. (2015). *Stay: Lessons my dogs taught me about life, loss and grace.* Tyndale House Publishers.

Casanova, L. (2018). *Grief, Grace and Gratitude – Transforming through your grief journey.* Lara Casanova.

Casanova, L. (2016). *Heartbreak, Healing and Happiness. Flourishing after a heartbreak.* Lara Casanova

Chase, M.J. (2013). *The Radical Practice of Loving Everyone: A four-legged approach to enlightenment.* Hay House, Inc.

Chase, M.J. (2011). *Am I Being Kind: How asking one simple question can change your life...and your world.* Hay House.

Chopra, D. (2010). *The Shadow Effect: Illuminating the hidden power of your true self.* HarperCollins Ebooks.

EXTRA RESOURCES

Coombes. M. (2016). *Sensing spirit.* Xou Pty Ltd.

Dalai Lama, Tutu, D., & Abrams, D. (2016). *The book of JOY. Lasting happiness in a changing world.* Hutchinson.

Dass, R. (2013). *Polishing the Mirror: How to live from your spiritual heart.* 1st edition. Sounds True.

De Angelis, B. (2015). *Soul Shifts: Transformative wisdom for creating a life of authentic awakening, emotional freedom and practical spirituality.* Hay House, Inc.

De Angelis, B. (2009). *Are You the One for Me?: Knowing who's right and avoiding who's wrong.* Dell.

Desai, P. (2014). *Discovering your Soul Signature: A 33-day path to purpose passion and joy.* Yellow Kite.

Dooley, M. (2014). *The Top Ten Things Dead People Want to Tell YOU.* 1st edition. Hay House, Inc.

Dowrick, S. (2012). *The Universal Heart: A practical guide to love.* Allen and Unwin.

Dyer, W.W. (2015). *I Can See Clearly Now.* Hay House, Inc.

Elliott, S.J. (2009). *Getting Past Your Breakup: How to turn a devastating loss into the best thing that ever happened to you.* Da Capo Press.

Fox, B. (2001). *Working Through Panic: Your step by step guide to overcoming panic/anxiety related disorders.* Prentice Hall.

Gilbert, E. (2007). *Eat, Pray, Love: One woman's search for everything across Italy, India and Indonesia.* 25th printing edition. Penguin (Non-Classics).

Greig, S, Hess M R. (2019). *The One and Only Wolfgang: From Pet Rescue to One Big Happy Family.* Zonderkidz.

Hale, M. (2013). *The Single Woman: Life, love, and a dash of sass.* Thomas Nelson.

Hassler, C. (2014). *Expectation Hangover: Overcoming disappointment in work, love, and life.* New World Library.

Hawn, R. (2015). *Heart Dog: Surviving the loss of your canine soulmate.* Roxanne Hawn.

Hay, L., & Holden, R. (2015). *Life Loves You: 7 spiritual practices to heal your life.* Hay House.

Hay, L.L. (1984). *You Can Heal Your Life.* 2nd edition. Hay House.

Hay, L.L. (2014). *You Can Heal Your Heart: Finding peace after a breakup, divorce, or death.* Hay House, Inc.

Hickman, M.W. (1994). *Healing After Loss: Daily meditations for working through grief.* 1st edition. William Morrow Paperbacks.

Holden, R. (2011). *Shift Happens!: How to live an inspired life... starting right now!* Revised edition. Hay House.

Jackson. L.L. (2015). *The light between us. Stories from heaven. Lessons for the living.* Century.

Jeffers, S. (2006). *Feel the Fear and Do It Anyway.* 20th anniversary edition. Ballantine Books.

Kipp, M. (2014). *Daily Love: Growing into grace.* Hay House.

Kirshenbaum, M. (1997). *Too Good to Leave, Too Bad to Stay: A step-by-step guide to help you decide whether to stay in or get out of your relationship.* Reprint Edition. Plume.

Kübler-Ross, E., & Kessler, D. (2014). *On grief & grieving: Finding the meaning of Grief through the Five Stages of Loss.* Scribner.

Extra Resources

Moutounet, G. (2017). *My Dog, My Guru: A Dog's Principles for a Happier Life.* Hay House UK.

Nichols, L. (2009). *No Matter What!: 9 steps to living the life you love.* 1st edition. Grand Central Life and Style.

Romeo, E. (2015). *Meet Your Soul: A powerful guide to connect with your most sacred self.* Hay House.

Rosen, R. (2011). *Spirited: Unlock your psychic self and change your life.* Reprint edition. Harper Perennial.

Silver, T. (2014). *Outrageous Openness: Letting the divine take the lead.* Atria Books.

Spencer, K. (2013). *Twelve Lessons.* The Lightworkers Academy.

Stosny, S. (2013). *Living and Loving after Betrayal: How to heal from emotional abuse, deceit, infidelity, and chronic resentment.* 1st edition. New Harbinger Publications.

Thomas, K.W. (2007). *Calling in "The One": 7 weeks to attract the love of your life.* Harmony.

Tolle, E. (2004). *The Power of Now: A guide to spiritual enlightenment.* Namaste Publishing.

Tracy, B. (1995). *Maximum Achievement: Strategies and skills that will unlock your hidden powers to succeed.* 1st fireside edition. Simon and Schuster.

Vanzant, I. (2002). *Living Through the Meantime: Learning to break the patterns of the past and begin the healing process.* Touchstone.

Virtue, D. (2013). *Assertiveness for Earth Angels: How to be loving instead of "Too Nice".* Hay House.

Virtue, D. (2015). *Don't Let Anything Dull Your Sparkle: How to break free of negativity and drama*. Hay House.

Virtue, D., & Van Praagh, J. (2013). *How to heal a grieving heart*. Hay House.

Williamson, M. (1996). *A Return to Love: Reflections on the principles of "A Course in Miracles"*. Reissue Edition. HarperOne.

Other Helpful Links

Grief support

- Beyond Blue Australia — Grief support — P: 1300 224 636 — https://www.beyondblue.org.au
- By My Side Counselling, Australia — Specialising in pet loss and grief — https://Bymysidecounselling.net.au
- Kids Helpline, Australia — Support and counselling — P: 1800 551 800 — https://kidshelpline.com.au/
- Center for Pet Loss Grief — Pet loss grief and support — https://centerforpetlossgrief.com
- Gary Roe: Author, Speaker, Grief Specialist — Caring for grieving hearts — https://www.garyroe.com
- Lifeline, Australia — Crisis support — P: 13 11 14 — https://www.lifeline.org.au
- Our Wonderful Pets — A place to honour your pet — http://www.ourwonderfulpets.com
- Pets and People — Pet loss and grief support counselling hotline — Australia P: 1300 431 450, New Zealand P: 0800 114 421 — https://petsandpeople.com.au
- Suicide Call Back Service, Australia — P: 1300 659 467 — https://www.suicidecallbackservice.org.au

- 🐾 The Association for Pet Loss and Bereavement – Pet bereavement counselling – https://www.aplb.org

Children's books

- 🐾 *Lifetimes: The beautiful way to explain death to children.* Written by Bryan Mellonie
- 🐾 *When Your Pet Dies: A Healing Handbook for Kids.* Written By Victoria Ryan and Illustrated by R W Alley.

Memorial plaques/stones

- 🐾 Talking Stones – https://talkingstones.com.au
- 🐾 Living existence metal artwork/Metal rusty heart – https://www.facebook.com/andosarts
- 🐾 Soul Trees – Biodegradable urns/Memorial trees – https://soultrees.com.au/product/product-bios-urn

Meditation apps

- 🐾 Calm – https://www.calm.com
- 🐾 Gaia – https://www.gaia.com
- 🐾 Headspace – https://www.headspace.com/headspace-meditation-app
- 🐾 Insight Timer – https://insighttimer.com

Other Helpful Links

Podcasts by Lara Casanova

- Amanda's Wellbeing Podcast – https://amandaswellbeingpodcast.com/lara-casanova
- Cat Explorer – https://catexplorer.co/podcast-entries/grieving-for-your-pet-with-lara-casanova-life-in-the-pink
- Kimberly Wilson podcast – https://kimberlywilson.com/podcasts/tranquility-du-jour-492-healing-heartbreak/
- My Instruction Manual – https://myinstructionmanual.com/2019/05/20/the-art-of-grief

Loss, Love and Lessons

"To call him a dog hardly seems to do him justice, though inasmuch as he had four legs, a tail and barked, I admit he was, to all outward appearances. But to those of us who knew him well, he was a perfect gentleman."

—Hermione Gingold

"It's just the most amazing thing to love a dog, isn't it? It makes our relationships with people seem as boring as a bowl of oatmeal."

— John Grogan

"My fashion philosophy is, if you're not covered in dog hair, your life is empty."

—Elayne Boosler

www.ingramcontent.com/pod-product-compliance
Lightning Source LLC
Chambersburg PA
CBHW071559080526
44588CB00010B/963